WAR CHILD

(1939-1945)

by

DIONE VENABLES

Edited by Guy Loftus

PUBLISHED by Finlay Publisher

Copyright © 2025 All rights reserved

ISBN: 978-1-0682117-1-3

BOOKS ALSO PUBLISHED BY DIONE

As D.G. FINLAY

Once Around the Sun

The Edge of Tomorrow

Watchman

The Grey Regard

Deadly Relations

Graven Image

The Killing Glance

As DIONE VENABLES

The Postscript Edition to Eric & Us, by Jacintha Buddicom

George Orwell: The Complete Poetry

Dione's War

Dione, by June, 1947

FOREWORD

If you don't like clowns (perhaps you even find them a little scary), then try not to look at them directly. Look closely instead at the face of a child watching, because then you will understand better what clowning is all about. You can apply the same legerdemain to war: we and future generations may never know what it is like to live through a world at war. But if you look closely at the life of one child whose existence was distorted by wartime, you will understand better what war is all about. Overlay that external conflagration with the child's own internal turmoil and you get closer to what *War Child* is all about.

War Child is Dione Venables' poignant and often shockingly candid memoir growing up in World War II from the moment Britain declared war in September

1939, to the celebrations of VE Day in May 1945. The *Child,* Dione (pronounced dai.uh.nee – to rhyme with Hermione)[1], takes us through eight vivid chapters, each offering an unique perspective as she is chivvied around London in an often futile attempt to shield her from the war's reach. We see the war initially through the eyes of a spirited nine-year-old desperate for her mother's approval, emerging five years later as a war-weary 14-year-old adolescent filled with new hope and fiery independence. She takes us through a global conflict expressed as a deeply personal journey of survival. In effect, *War Child* explores the collision of three wars: the external horror of global war, the domestic turmoil within her family, and her private, internal war of identity and puberty. With each collision, a piece of her childhood is lost forever, sometimes violently (Dione narrowly escaped with her life three times in this period).

Dione Venables died in 2023 at the generous age of 92, having written *Dione's War* in 2016 aged eighty-six. Reaching into childhood at that age coherently and accurately was not easy for Dione, requiring some encouragement, particularly reliving the awful events covered in chapter 7. What emerged was a very poignant and often intimate account written for family and close friends only, with a lot of familial references both historical and contemporary. As with all passing generations, there was content that Dione didn't want to share more widely when she was alive, but actively encouraged me to publish when she had gone. *War Child* is an editorial adaptation of *Dione's War*, with care

---

[1] Few people have been able to pronounce her name throughout her life, which set her apart from other children. Those who could were seen as closer to her than those who couldn't, which was even more obvious in adulthood.

taken to preserve her voice but with a degree of resequencing and deletions to maintain narrative flow. *War Child* also includes some insertions from an earlier account written by Dione in 1996, hurriedly put together to exorcise her grief when her then husband, John, had just died. I was her editor in 1996 and 20 years later in 2016 and am her editor for *War Child*, so accountability stops with me. What I hope has emerged is a much tighter account of her war experiences without the loss of authenticity or impact. Her very candid story is ultimately about resilience, about how Dione asserted herself in a world where her identity was constantly under threat, a journey many of us can identify with. Her journey is both harrowing and hopeful but demonstrates that you don't have to be a hero to be heroic - you only have to choose not to be a victim.

My love and thanks go to my siblings Nicky and Sally, who gave their total support for publication, to cousin Paul Webb for his help untangling memory, to Douglas Kerr for continuous encouragement, Quentin Kopp and Steven Bloemendaal for their moral support, to Darcy Moore for last-minute proof reading, Richard Barrett for being the first spec reader and to my wife Pauline for her patience, and who reviewed the text to cover my many blind spots.

Guy Loftus, Hampton, London, May 2025

TABLE OF CONTENTS

LIST OF ILLUSTRATIONS

CHAPTER ONE

The Phoney War

We had almost finished packing that morning after church, because our school trunks had to be sent off in advance and Carter Patterson, the removals and cartage people, were collecting them the following day. Moo always struggled with those final moments before the trunk lids were closed, the latches clipped down and the locks turned, worried that she had forgotten some vital item without which her daughters could not possibly live. The labels had to be double-checked this term, to ensure that Junie's trunk would be off-loaded for the first time at the Senior School entrance, while my old blue cabin trunk, a relic of past grand-parents' voyages to and from Australia, would join the pile of luggage at the glass-doored entrance to the Junior School arcade. We were always assisted in our packing by Sally, our wire-haired fox terrier with yellow and black markings on a white coat and an elegant little pointed French beard, who had appeared at the beginning of the Summer holidays in 1937 and quickly became a cherished and much cuddled member of the family. She slept on my bed, and generally attached herself to me, whatever I was up to. I loved the feel of her coat, the

1

warmth of her wet pink nose, the sheer love in her bright eyes.

1 - "Moo" (Florence Gordon-Finlay), 1916

The Winter term of September 1939 would be a momentous one; the uncertainty of another great war hanging over the Nation, the beginning of the school year, and Junie, now thirteen, was moving with her class up into the lofty heights of the Senior school, which meant that I would be really on my own for the first time. I would be transferred from the pink cosiness and floral comfort of the Babies' Dormitory, where I had lived for six years, to the more austere reality of the Junior Dorm; white curtains and bed covers; polished wood floors; no toys allowed on the beds. I was afraid of the unknown element in so much change, of leaving home again, of leaving Moo again, of being sick in the car. In the middle of picking a corner of my battered blue trunk where a tiny thread of the enamelled canvas had come loose, and pushing Sally out from where she was doing her best to unpack it, I heard us being called. There was a sharp urgency to Pa's usually quiet voice.

"Junie - Dooks. You must hear this announcement from the Prime Minister. Hurry up!"

We rushed headlong down the broad, shadowed hallway of the London flat, Sally, sensing a game, leaping joyously between us, into the drawing-room where the wireless crackled and hissed and a tired, sonorous voice had already begun to speak. There was something about

Neville Chamberlain's voice that was holding my parents in their chairs like wax effigies, sitting forward as though they could not get close enough to the wireless, to Chamberlain himself. Pa's usually good-humoured face was set in stone, the deep lines on either side of his mouth dark runnels between which his moustache drooped over the restless mobility of his mouth. Today his lips were sealed so tightly that they had almost disappeared.

"I am speaking to you from the Cabinet Room of 10 Downing Street. This morning the British Ambassador in Berlin, Neville Henderson, handed the German Government a final note, stating that unless we heard from them by 11 o'clock, that they were prepared at once to withdraw their troops from Poland, a state of war would exist between us. I have to tell you now that no such undertaking has been received, and that consequently this country is at war with Germany."

The hesitant, strained voice with its carefully clipped vowels continued to spell out the situation of a country only just beginning to recover from the First World War a bare twenty years before, but Pa did not appear to be listening. He bent his head and his shoulders shook. Moo, her face drained of all colour, leaned over and gripped his arm and for a moment they seemed to freeze together, the broadcast ignored, the crackly atmospherics of our wireless the only accompaniment to their emotion. Junie went to Pa and put her arms round him. It was not necessary to understand what the Prime Minister was still saying but, whatever it meant, it had dealt Pa a mortal blow and she could not bear to see a long tear slide down the side of his nose and hang for a moment before melting into his moustache. I looked at the three of them, a triple unit of pain with their arms around each other and I wanted to go to Moo and give her my own brand of comfort and love for whatever was causing her such agony, but I knew she might turn away and shrug me off, gently but firmly, and tell me 'not to cling so…….' I sat on the end of the sofa and tried to listen and learn the reason for what was happening to my parents. The voice, its resonance fading and surging, pressed on and finally came to an end………

"Now may God bless you all. May he defend the Right. It is the evil things that we shall be fighting against - brute force, bad faith, injustice, oppression and persecution - and against them I am certain that the Right will prevail."

Sonorous funereal music followed and as Pa reached over to turn the 'off '-switch the telephone began to ring in the hall and Junie jumped up and went to answer it. Her voice was too soft for me to hear what she was saying but Moo and Pa stared at each other, their faces still stricken from the broadcast. I inched across towards Moo and laid a hand on her arm, where her cream silk blouse cuff became her wrist, needing the feel of her, the comfort of the warm fragrance of her violet-soothed skin.

2 - *"Pa" (Alan Gordon-Finlay) 1914*

"It's for you." said Junie to Pa at the drawing-room door. He gave a deep sigh and pulled himself up out of the chair, running a finger along Moo's upturned cheek as he passed her. I slid into the chair beside my mother and put my arms round her as

Junie came to join us. We sat without saying a word, Sally curled up against my back, and listened to the quiet rumble of Pa's voice, his long silences and brief responses, and then the 'ting' of the bell as he put the receiver back on its hook.

"I have to go." He said in the doorway. "I'll phone you when I know what is going on but I might be late. You know how it is….."

Moo certainly knew how it was. She was long used to him being summoned away at odd hours. They had both known that he would be very occupied, should War be declared. At this point I should try and clarify the fact that I simply do not know what Pa was engaged in at this time. Indeed, I had not been aware of anything that he was doing as I was growing up. The fragments that come to mind are the presence in the London flat of miniature parachutes with weights, which I am told were part of the experiments he was engaged in concerning parachute shells. The other subject I know he was engaged in was the system of de-magnetising ships. Pa's attention was, on the 3rd September 1939, focused on a system called de-gaussing, which would ensure the floating magnetic mines that Germany was about to scatter all over the English Channel, would not explode on contact with a metal hull. From this, I have to assume that Pa was at that time employed, either in the Army or within the War Office, by the Government in some way.

There is one clear impression from those days that I still have with me, and that is the feeling of dread that followed the sound of the first air raid siren, warning the public of approaching enemy aircraft. The first of these warnings happened shortly after the Prime Minister's speech, when all the sirens went off in London, and in all the cities of Britain, to show the people what to expect. We were instructed that warning of the approach of enemy aircraft would be heard with the siren rising and falling for two minutes, during which time we must all take cover. The All Clear was sounded when that danger was past, the siren wailing its message on one shrill note for another two minutes. My terror was extreme when I first heard the warning because there came a clear image into my head of the entire sky suddenly filled with parachutists being dropped out of the blue canopy above us. They would all be dressed in scarlet jackets, black trousers, tall black bearskins on their heads - rifles in their hands, bayonets at the ready. *We were all going to be stabbed to death!* I can only assume that I had this vivid image in my mind because the only soldiers I had ever seen outside a story book, apart from Pa when he wore khaki, were the guards at Buckingham Palace, a familiar sight to all Londoners. That is how they were dressed, though I do not quite see where the bayonet-primed rifles came from. I do know that I fastened myself to Moo like a limpet, resisting all attempts to be dis-engaged, and she must have realised how frightened I was because I do not remember her shaking me off just then. That oddly 'Toy Town' image has always stayed with me, and I am quite fond of it these days because it was created when I was so young, not quite nine years old, and not at all in charge of my vivid imagination. That took time to control.

Junie and I were not prepared for the sinister wail which came out of nowhere; starting low, climbing to a shrill shrieking wail and then dipping and rising for two whole minutes. Moo shooed us into the hall, called to Maisie, our daily maid, to join us, closed all the doors so that we were sealed into a windowless corridor, and we sat in gloomy shadow, listening to the tick of the grandfather clock, talking in curiously muted voices and waiting for the All Clear.

"Will we have to go back to school?" I asked hopefully, trying to see the bright side of things, and thinking how blissful it would be to stay here in my own comfortable bed beside Junie's, with Sally-dog curled up beside me, a furry hot water bottle, instead of facing life without her in the long cold Junior Dorm. Moo planted a kiss on the top of my head.

"Of course you will, Silly. School is the best place for you both at this time, especially as it is so far from London. You'll have to go with the Batch, though, because Pa will need the car unless he gets a unit car and a driver."

The All Clear sounded its clarion call of reassurance and, relieved that we had not been attacked, we scattered to continue packing, making lunch, writing letters, and, without doubt, I would have been happily hugging the news that we were not driving back to school that term.

The Batch! Oh Joy…. I had only once before joined the school group taking the train from Charing Cross Station to Warrior Square, St. Leonards, but what fun that had been. No travel-sick qualms in the pit of the stomach, caused by the fumes of our Rover's engine exhaust. Twenty or more children in a reserved carriage with three nuns to look after us as we sped past the squalid backs of Deptford through to Orpington, bursting out of the grime and murky air, past Lewisham and at last to the fresh Kent breezes of Sevenoaks and

Tunbidge Wells. The Batch was the most exciting way to start the term because it gave new arrivals at the school a chance to meet some of the children they would be living and learning with. On top of the roll call, which started as soon as the train began to move, the nuns would produce thermoses of wonderful hot beef tea from big wicker baskets, which they poured into Bakelite cups, and we were each given a small package containing a fresh bloater paste or sardine sandwich, and an apple. This was a picnic feast, and a very good move to break the shyness of the new children. It kept us occupied so that, by the time we settled down and watched the countryside flying by outside the train windows, we were well on our way to the coast.

The Batch was where friendships often began for the new children, but Junie and I were old hands, having been right through the Junior school, and we already had our special friends to greet and to compare our holiday adventures with. That day remains quite clear to me because even I, who was not quite nine years old but often listened to Pa and Moo discussing World Affairs, was all too aware that much of the World we knew was changing around us with every breath we took. Mind you, because we were children with no experience of the agonizing pressures of War, I was inclined to regard it as the start of a *Great Adventure*; who knew what was in store for us in the future? Maybe we would have to go and hide in the Scottish mountains where no enemy would ever find us - all kinds of wild and wonderful images flooded my mind while those around me were wearing longer and longer faces.

The beginnings and ends of our school terms were what defined Junie's and my lives, which had for the last five years, been neatly divided into four sections:

School term/ Beginning and end of term/ School holidays/ Travel between Switzerland and London.

I have no idea why our school group on the train was always called The Batch (I always intended to try and discover its source from the historian who is in charge of St. Leonards-Mayfield today) but the dictionary says that it indicates a group; a batch of bread loaves, a batch of Christmas trees – so 'a batch of schoolgirls' has a certain resonance and logic! I do remember the strict control our three guardian nuns kept on us though. The carriage, mostly reserved for us, was a corridor train with six compartments to each carriage. Six girls to each compartment and one set aside for the nuns and their picnic baskets meant that a couple of compartments were used by the general public. They must have been glad to reach their destinations when you consider the noise level and general dashing-around of twenty small girls who have not seen each other all summer! But this of course is a different age we are looking at and I don't think we did dash around much during the journey, but were encouraged to sit quietly in our seats and not raise our voices. Children dashing around happened in the next generation when we, who had been so over-controlled, were much more permissive with our own children.

When we arrived at Warrior Square Station, we were briskly removed from the train, lined up in twos and marched out of the station, up the steep hill, turn right into Magdalen Road and there, as the road sloped downwards again towards the sea, were the school gates - open and waiting for us on the left of the road, with the restless sea, winking blue and sparkling a welcome, straight ahead. I do not remember how Junie and I parted that day in 1939, but one moment she was there and the next moment I, in my Juniors group, turned into the open glass Arcade doors of the Junior school and the Seniors moved on up the drive towards the main building and the school chapel – and were gone. The change had begun.

Our return to school was a couple of days after War was declared. Moo had stopped telling everyone that if Chamberlain had made his announcement a week later, she and Sally-dog would have returned to Lausanne and been separated from her entire family for the whole War. As it was, she remained in the flat in Kensington Court that Pa had been left by his aunt Toddie in 1936, and which we, and other family members used as our base when we came over from Switzerland.

Quite apart from the strangeness of *not* being in the Babies Dormitory (I had been there for six years, but my 'home' was now a bed on the left side of the Junior Dorm, the third bed along from the bathrooms. There was a new girl on my left and I forget who was on the other side. It all felt strange and impersonal and the new girl next to me sat on her bed, head bowed, swinging her legs and looking miserable. I wish I could remember conversations but I cannot, and am not going to invent things we might have said, but I do remember feeling sorry for her, and it was the beginning of my friendship with Patricia Holroyd.

At the age of three, I was the youngest pupil that the school had ever accepted and I still cannot think how my parents persuaded the nuns to agree to take a small child, let alone had ever been separated from her family. The nuns did their very best with me in those early years, when I was still too young for

3 - Dione was sent to board at the age of three

even the baby class. The result of over-indulgence at such an early age by the whole Community was a pretty precocious child whose talents were often hidden behind a wall of willfulness and rebellion. I was not where I wanted to be - which was close to my mother. I never quite managed to stop looking for Moo's love, and right to the end of her life I never quite found it. Moo did not have it in her to understand *why* I kept looking for her approval, and to love me, *despite* my early indiscretions.

At the beginning of the Christmas term in 1939, the declaration of war concealed a period of uncertainty, which felt like a great black hole that we were gradually being sucked into. The school was constantly visited by groups of officials to check that safety orders for all schools were being carried out. There was little time to miss Junie because the school was being prepared for bomb attacks as the impressive Victorian buildings were in a spread of seventeen acres at the top of a hill, across the valley in which Hastings town had been built, looking across to Hastings Castle. So we would be a sitting target for enemy bombers and the nuns had already been advised to move us all to a safer site, or

11

close the school altogether. In the meantime, sandbags were piled up, two or three thick, round the long glass panels of the Junior School's Entry Arcade, windows were criss-crossed with strong brown sticky paper, and The Tunnel was prepared to become our bomb shelter.

The Tunnel was a strange place, full of shadows and dry fusty air. It was the underground connection between the Junior and Senior Schools and ran from the music room corridor in the Junior School, under the broad gravel drive, and emerged near the front door of the Senior School. Many of the younger children were frightened of this long dark place, even though there were electric lights every few yards along its curved ceiling. Often some of these lights blew a fuse and there were pools of darkness through which it was wise to run as fast as possible in case something came up out of the black unknown and swept you away.

With War in mind, school benches were brought down to line the tunnel on both sides, and the exits were sandbagged on both sides of the doors. Its crypt-like odour gradually shifted as the wood of the varnished benches began to absorb the musty atmosphere, and it somehow seemed a little less frightening, a little more like the smell of our classrooms. All the same, it was always a truly scary, almost too thrilling experience, scuttling through the Tunnel alone, with black shadows reaching out, billowing between pale yellow blobs of ceiling light and listening to the clatter of our shoes on stone and the thunder of our hearts in our ears.

As the Junior School had to use the tunnel several times a day, we all felt moved by it in one way or another and experienced fear, excitement or delicious daring-do as we clattered down the steps from the music room corridor and into its murky gloom. Sometimes you could just see the hall light at the other end, but there were often occasions if a bulb had blown when you could not, and we rushed forward like the nursery rhyme's blind mice, with a hand on the shoulder of the person in front. We used the Tunnel for going to Church (twice or three times a day), for going to the refectory (four times a day), and for the School Hall for plays, music and dancing practice. In addition to that, you scuttled through on your own if you were sent to the San (sanitorium), to see Reverend Mother, to attend choir practice or to run errands for the nuns. I have often thought I should try and discover when the Tunnel was built, as it may well have been some time after the two large school buildings and the beautiful Pugin chapel went up in 1848.

One day, during the second week of term, three uniformed men from the Civil Defence arrived and set up a table in the refectory, piling it with brown cardboard boxes. Inside every box was a rubber gas mask and each of us was fitted with one of these suitably air-tight devices. They were made of strong-smelling black rubber with a celluloid (Perspex) window to see through, and canvas straps that went over the head and fastened tightly behind the left ear with a metal buckle, which invariably pulled ones' hair. There was white talc inside and you put your chin in first and then slid the whole thing over your face, where it sat tightly, gripping the flesh of your cheeks and jaw on either side. When you breathed in, the air was drawn in through a circular filter nozzle pressed against your nose and mouth, giving the wearer a comic 'Miss Piggy' look, and when you breathed out, the air was expelled on each side of the mask along both cheeks. My trouble was that I was asthmatic and I simply could not breathe in that awful rubber-smelling contraption.

I think that this is the first moment that I actually remember the presence in my mind of an invisible companion called Ian, who was saying to me while I was trying not to put that gas mask on, that I must try because it might save my life at some point. "Naughty girl." I was scolded. "You are just being difficult. Here…put it on yourself if it will make you feel happier. Nonsense, child - of course you can breathe. These masks have been designed by experts - and they are for your safety, you know." Eventually, after more tears and much wheezing – and encouraging sounds from Ian in my head, I managed to put on the horrible black thing, having spat on the celluloid window as directed, rubbing the surface with my forefinger to stop it misting with my breath. I even learned to breathe slowly and deeply and to ignore the painful tightness in my chest that the whole performance gave me. In the end, I only had to put on the gas mask one more time and that was when a very smart bright metallic green extra filter arrived for us all, which had to be strapped onto the existing filter to keep out a new sort of gas that the Germans had just invented. As long as I didn't have to wear it, I became quite fond of my smelly old gas mask in its neat green waterproof case. Junie had a blue one. Looking back, it occurs to me that I had this same gas mask in 1944, when we were hit by a Flying Bomb, as I had been given at the beginning in 1939. As we all did a lot of growing in those four years, it would have been much too small for me, had I needed to put it on at the age of 13.

Two strange table-like contraptions appeared in the school grounds; one in the Junior School playground and the other outside the Senior School Common Room. They were pieces of wood maybe three feet square, fixed at an angle so that their whole surface could be seen, and nailed to a waist-high wooden post. They were painted a very bright iridescent yellowy-green so that you could not ignore them. We were told that they were an early warning against a gas attack, and that if the colour changed to red, we were to put on our gas masks *at once*. I never did get to know what sort of red to expect, had this happened, but it never did. The whole of the British Isles was peppered with these Gas warning plaques, in country and town, at crossroads, on walls and against trees. I wonder whether any of them survive today?

4 - Boarders at Maidwell School testing gas masks (left) and dormitory fire-practice, 1939 (photographed by Geoffrey Loftus)

Soon after the issue of gas masks, we were given identity cards. I don't have mine any more, although I still have some of my old junior clothing coupons for the under 18s, and two ration cards of Moo's and Junie's that we discovered in Moo's papers after she died. However, I still remember that my identity card was pale blue and my National Registration number was: EIDD 2126.

The Convent of the Holy Child Jesus must have been a really good school because there is so much of its daily routine that I remember today with pleasure. For a start, the food was wonderful. As I left St. when I was ten, it surely says something for the quality of the food to be forever remembered. But it really was first class. I'm quite hazy about breakfasts except that their porridge was lovely and creamy. Then in winter we had beef tea for 'elevenses' and if ever I drink beef tea – and that is very rarely these days – the flavour and delicate aroma bring back an immediate image of elevenses at St. Leonards, feeding a piece of digestive biscuit to Connor the cockatoo and trying not to get my fingers nipped. Lunch was always a feast with plenty of fresh vegetables from the kitchen gardens and on Fridays, fish caught by the Hastings fishing fleet. My favourite pudding was rice pudding – but only the St. Leonards version. The fact that the great pans of overcooked rice pudding meant that they were brown and treacly made the whole rice pudding absolutely scrumptious. Even the rice was brown and tasted sweet and creamy like soft toffee. And as for the crunchy scrapings round the side of the pan - aaaaagghh! My mouth is watering at the mere thought. Meat was fresh and cooked in a variety of ways so that we all ate every single thing that was put on our plates. Except for me, of course.

I had, for some reason I cannot remember, become very thin by 1938 and the doctor prescribed a carton of double cream for me to consume every day. Instead of putting it on my pudding at lunch time, as you'd have thought would be the natural way to give it to me, I had to eat it with a spoon from the carton after supper every evening. It was always sour by the time it reached me (they did not put preservatives into anything in those days and the carton would have been sitting all day in a larder rather than in a fridge) and I had to struggle with a whole pot of rich double *sour* cream by the spoonful - and of course it made me sick. Every evening for what must have been at least a week, I sat in the refectory alone at a long table with this dreadful pot of sour cream to swallow - and every evening I ended up by being sick. I don't remember *exactly* how long I was made to suffer this torture, but I think the San matron took pity on me in the end, and told my parents that I was getting more dehydrated than helped by this foolish 'food supplement' and that they were going to have a really sick daughter if they did not give instructions to stop this particular diet. I've never been able to stomach thick, let alone *sour,* cream since that day. The loss of weight continued and then I had chest pains. "Whatever will you think up next?" sighed Moo, as though my condition was my fault. It turned out that I had a heart murmur, which was not really understood in those days and I was labeled "cardiac risk."

I had my ninth birthday on the 20th October 1939, and as Junie and I always had our birthdays during term time, Pa was able to get time off (I still do not know what he was doing then) and he and Moo drove down to the school from London and took us out for a birthday tea to the Pilgrim's Rest at Battle. The Pilgrim's Rest is still there - very much smaller than my early memory, but the same lovely old ancient beamed building in the shadow of Battle Abbey, where the Battle of Hastings was fought in 1066, and which is, at the time of writing this, a well-respected girls school. I was only allowed to invite three friends to the Birthday tea party because we could not fit any more into the Rover - which Pa had nick-named 'Winnie The Poo', because of its sick-making petrol fumes - and there were crackers and balloons, plates of sandwiches, little cakes, jellies and ice cream as well as their fabled birthday cake. We drove back to school with our insides bursting and our heads hanging out of the car windows in case we felt sick! It was the last birthday celebration I had, for the War was upon us and it would not be long before rationing bit into our diets, and my skinniness would be forgotten since we were all going to be short of food before long.

The first time the sirens went, warning us of approaching enemy aircraft, was about two weeks into the term and France, having declared War at the same time as Britain, had just begun an offensive against Germany's Western border. We were in the middle of making our beds before morning prayers. Sister Burkmanns came whisking into the dormitory, black veil flying out behind her. "Come along, children." She called. "Straight down to the Tunnel. Leave your beds. Bring your gas masks. HURRY." We made for the door in an orderly stampede - twelve of us in that long room, pushing at each other as we tumbled down the stairs, rushed through the school hall, up through two classrooms, along the arcade and the passage by the music rooms. Another nun waited for us there and she pulled us up, comforted those who looked frightened with a smile and a joke, and aimed us down the stairs and into the dimly lit Tunnel. The seniors were already coming down from the other end and it seemed that we were full up in no time, with the almost invisible black-robed nuns floating through the opaque shadows between us and the narrow pathway of our knees and feet.

That first raid lasted over an hour, during which time the air became thick and I began to cough, and because we did not have inhalers in those days, I was only able to breathe into a camphor pad, which was meant to help but often did not. It quickly became clear to the nuns that we needed more air in the Tunnel, or else the children were at risk of suffocation if we were all pressed together in that confined space for too long. They started on a plan to build another air raid shelter for the seniors and some of the nuns, but it was never completed. Instead, it was decided that the whole school, being the most outstanding landmark in St Leonards/Hastings, apart from Hastings Castle and the elegant Art Deco block of flats, Marina Court, was at risk of being targeted and bombed. By the end of the Christmas term, the school's trustees were out, scouring England for a suitable place to move 168 children to a place of safety.

During that term, a wireless appeared in the refectory so that each day, while we were having our meals, we listened to the soon familiar voices of Alvar Liddell and Stuart Hibbert reading the BBC News at one o'clock and six o'clock. National News made a great change from the usual things that children, especially small girls, listened to on the Wireless at that time – which was mainly Uncle Mac presenting Children's Hour and every Sunday joining in the very catchy song that Ovaltine put out to advertise their promotions club, *The Ovaltineys*.

> '*We are the Ovaltineys,*
> *Happy boys and girls.*

WAR CHILD

Make your request, we'll not refuse you
We are here just to amuse you…'

I realised for the first time what it meant to be living on an island with sea all round us, and in that sea the first battles were already taking place. The German Navy's U-boats lost no time in attacking our British Merchant ships which daily brought in vital food and supplies to keep the population and the War Effort going. There was an initial heavy loss of ships, men and supplies but the Royal Navy was hard at work and reports streamed in of one battle after another in every direction, from the Channel, down into the Mediterranean Sea and across the Atlantic. After a period when volunteers were asked to join the three armed services, it became obvious that more were needed and every able man between the ages of twenty-two and forty-four was being called-up for military service, and this soon began to include women. Later the minimum age was dropped to seventeen and a half and the maximum up to fifty. I decided that I was going to join up as soon as I was old enough to become a motor-cycle dispatch rider, carrying precious documents and life-changing messages to the Great and The Good. Junie thought she'd like to be a War Artist.

Following the Christmas Nativity play that year, the two school choirs assembled on stage to sing to their audience. The last number in the programme was the first solo I ever sang. I was one of the smaller children, even for the Junior choir. They dressed me up with a dark blue raincoat, wellington boots and a tin helmet with ARP stencilled on the front in white, borrowed from one of the smaller air raid wardens in Magdalen Road. I stood centre-stage with my gas mask over my shoulder and a Union Jack flag in one hand and sang

"There'll Always Be An England." This was a highly patriotic song that had been composed for a film in 1939 and which the young singer Vera Lynn had begun, since the beginning of the War, to sing when she visited and sang for the ever-increasing military camps all over the country. Soon she would be flying round the World, singing for soldiers, sailors and airmen in all the countries that were supporting The United Kingdom and its Allies. But that was later. In December 1939, it was a small girl in an over-sized tin helmet, who sang it with the Junior School Choir as back-up for the Christmas performance of the School's Nativity Play, followed by a choral medley of ballads and carols. The audience was made up of parents and the people of Hastings and St.. They stood and cheered with National pride and zeal at the end, when the curtain came down. The auditorium was more-or-less in darkness as all lights were directed onto the stage so I could really see nothing during the performance, apart from movement like a great wave breaking through the shrouded hall. But the energy of the clapping was unmistakable. The lights were switched on, the audience rose to its feet and raised the roof. The Junior School Choir (and a small girl) had hit exactly the right patriotic note at that emotional moment. It was through that solo that I came to the attention of our choirmaster, Mr Savory.

I cannot remember much about Christmas 1939. We met up with some cousins who lived in Kensington Square, next door to the old Convent of the Assumption, and celebrated in a very sombre and low-key way, the adults feeling that we could hardly celebrate the birth of Christ when a new generation of our young men were once more being asked to die for their country and for us! So we all became rather devout at that time.

The beautiful Catholic church of Our Lady of Victories in Kensington had been destroyed by incendiary bombs on the 13th September, not long after we had returned to St. Leonards, so we saw the New Year in, in the same quiet fashion and none of us waited up to hear the bells of St. Mary Abbott's church because all church bells had stopped ringing across the land, Parliament having decreed that they were only to be rung as a warning of Invasion or for the Celebration of Victory.

Junie and I, quite old enough now to look after our own clothes, sewed buttons on our school uniforms, washing and repairing where necessary and then laid everything out on our beds so that Moo, (and Sally-dog, nose into everything) could check that they were in good order to be packed, ready for the Easter term. I expect that Pa's military training had some influence there, or maybe his meticulous batman, Glass, of his younger years who had looked after Pa for some time until well after Junie was born, and had trained Moo in the duties of an officer's wife. She had been very young and inexperienced in all household issues in those days. There must have been a dozen little 'short cuts' in the domestic world that Glass taught Moo who, having been born in India, where there was help in the household to do the smallest chore, had not been reared to roll up her sleeves and set-to, under any circumstances. When Nanny Betty Brimble was with us she had taught me a lot about how to ensure that a button stayed on; how to darn a sock without lumps at the edges; practical patching; letting skirts up and down (Moo always bought a size too big so that we had more time to grow into our clothes) and taking tucks in and out as we changed shape. These alterations were mostly for me because I always inherited Junie's clothes, ensuring that Moo, ever careful with money, only had to shop for one daughter. As I was nearly five years younger than Junie, it meant that quite a lot of nipping and tucking had to be done when she outgrew anything. I was not at all aware, when I was growing up, that this might not have been the norm in every household, nor can I recall ever longing for something of my very own. Trying to emulate Junie's neat and perfect stitching was not easy, but in time I became quite good with my needle and was eventually acknowledged as the Family Champion Sock Darner, a task I really enjoyed.

By the end of the school holidays, Pa was, as nearly always by then, away on duty and so once again we joined the Batch at Charing Cross and rumbled out of London and away from a solitary, abandoned Moo, to start the 1940 Spring Term. We knew that the school had plenty of plans for our entertainment because we had the Annual Spring Picnic to look forward to, if the darkening situation of the German advance into Denmark, Norway and then Belgium that Spring did not make this a distant memory. Although Hastings was actually frighteningly close to the French and Belgian coasts and the nuns must have been desperately planning our removal from our vulnerable hilltop position, we knew nothing of the withdrawal of the Allied Expeditionary Force, which was then being steadily pushed back and back towards the English Channel.

The Battle of Dunkirk, also known as The Miracle of Dunkirk, involving the evacuation of some 330,000 British and Allied troops, happened over the period 26th May to the 4th June 1940, less than seventy miles across the Channel from Hastings. It was to be one of the most moving and emotional 'victories in defeat' that happened in the 2nd World War when it became known that our armies were being squeezed towards the coast by Germany and her allies, and the bulk of our Navy was too far away in other battle sectors to effectively evacuate such a huge body of men. A call for sea-worthy boats went out all round the coasts and cities of southern Britain, even as far inland as London, and a great fleet of small ships, ferries, private yachts, motor boats and little sailing boats began to assemble along the Kent coastal ports. Code-named Operation Dynamo, it fanned out across the Channel to the threatened French coast and along the Dunkirk shoreline. The small vessels gathered in 338,226 tired, wounded and sometimes traumatised troops off the beaches, and brought them back to England. It was an act of supreme courage, showing the affection and National pride that Britain had for its beleaguered armies and her allies. There are today countless individual stories being carefully recorded, relating to the bravery of the men who steered and sailed their vessels, from channel ferries to rowing boats, in order to save the lives of their countrymen. Many were lost at sea, targeted by the German air force, but more than 330,000 British, Canadian, French, Polish, Belgian and Dutch lives were successfully rescued and brought back to Britain to fight and eventually win the final offensives.

While the World was changing before our eyes less than a hundred miles away, we children at school on the East coast, facing France, were still unaware of what was happening on the vast continent of Europe. This period of what was almost a 'stand-off' was referred to as 'The Phoney War', but at this time the Royal Navy were beginning to lay floating mines in Norwegian waters just as Germany invaded Denmark and Norway. On the other side of the World in America, British actress Vivian Leigh won an Oscar for her performance in *Gone With The Wind*. At the convent, the nuns were planning our Annual Spring Picnic. There were actually two Spring picnics at the end of the spring term or the start of the summer term, one for the Junior School and one for the Seniors, and the Spring 1940 picnic at Fairlight Glen would be the first time that Junie quite remote and superior by then in the Senior School, would not be there to ensure that I did not fall out of a tree or wander away to the distant beach path down to the cove and the sea.

That beautiful sunny day, a day when so much violence was happening so close to our shores, is a clear memory of sheer delight, and was actually the last one the school organised at Fairlight Glen. Avoiding the war meant that plans were already advanced for the whole school to be evacuated to distant Torquay - and very many years later the nuns would have been distressed to learn that Fairlight Glen and its beach became a 21st century haven for nudist bathing. On that May day in 1940 though, it was the first time that we could all relax and enjoy our surroundings because, back in St. Leonards, the whole of the school, both Junior and Senior school buildings, was being 'fortified' and made as bomb-proof as our nuns could manage, in case they could not get us away to safety before the country was invaded by that ever-advancing, triumphal Axis Army across the Channel. This 'fortifying' business meant that classes were disrupted with the banging and bustle of elderly workmen (the young men had all gone to fight) shoring-up the larger windows with wood and banks of sandbags, with some entrances being blocked-off and others strengthened with more sandbags. We could not go anywhere, either inside or outside the school, without our gas masks hanging over our shoulders, and woe betide anyone who left hers anywhere or, even worse, lost it! Inside the lid of my gasmask case my name and address were printed, and every morning I took the mask out of its box and cleaned it with a damp cloth, usually my own face flannel which had the best surface, although I was always scolded if I was discovered using it. A soft handkerchief was the prescribed cloth. When it was dried, it had to have a dusting of talcum so that it would be easy to slip on and off.

The Juniors piled into two, or maybe there were three coaches which, in those days, we called *charabancs*. I believe this was a 19th century term for an open coach with bench seats, which, when locomotives began to appear on the roads, became known as a bus or autobus. Anyway, it was the beginning of the great Spring outdoor adventure and the mere sight of the buses lined up on the gravel drive outside the arcade doors on a bright and sunny morning, was enough to sweep away all the fears of bombs, invasion and War which were beginning to filter into our heads and to haunt us all.

In the Spring term we had to have a couple of our summer uniform dresses with us in case of hot weather and so we were allowed to wear these with our blazers. All the teaching staff were required to start their teaching careers at the sister convent in Oxford (Cherwell Edge) to take degrees in whatever subjects they later taught. The result has always been an enviable quality of education at St. Leonards-Mayfield. The fact that I have any education at all is a tremendous example of the nuns' dedication because, having started my education at the age of three years and eleven months, by the time I grew into the age where lessons began, I was not inclined to take much notice. Gradually I came to love anything to do with English, Music and Art - but could not be persuaded to apply myself to anything else at all. Indeed, I grew up to be fairly proficient in these three subjects - and very little else.

I suppose I remember that wonderful picnic day because of the sense of serenity and contentment it gave us all, the nuns included. It seems to me that every one of us enjoyed that day so much because none of us would have another day like it until after the war was over. We had two nuns in each *charabanc*, and the driver, who helped to offload the bulky whicker picnic hampers, trestle tables, heavy water containers, boxes of china, rugs, umbrellas and bags to collect the rubbish at the end of the day. The food was, without exception, marvellous - sandwiches of soft fresh bread and a variety of fillings to die for. I always made a dive for the egg sandwiches because they had lovely peppery watercress mixed in with the buttery egg filling and I would have eaten them till I burst, had someone not kept an eye to ensure that I, and other greedy girls, did not grab more than our fair share. There were slices of cold quiche, and delicious chicken legs, which had been marinaded in something that was surely invented in heaven. I do not think that food ever tasted any better for me than the food we ate at that wonderful school.

At the beginning of the day, as soon as we arrived at Fairlight Glen, tumbled out of the *charabanc* and were all gathered round Mother Mary Joan, Picnic Leader that year, she and her two assistants gave us all a cold drink of home-made lemon-barley water, and then instructed us in what she wanted us to go hunting for; particular plants, flowers, and tree leaves etc. We all had exercise books and a pencil case filled with crayons for drawing, colouring, flower-pressing and writing up our finds. We had to stay within sound of the picnic area, keep our gasmasks with us - and we were not, under any circumstances, to speak to any strangers, should we come across any.

The previous year, when I was eight, I had been searching for a particular kind of pebble along the path that wound down to the beach steps, when a man had approached me from the stairway. He had nothing on at all. I had never seen a naked man before. It was the expression on his face not his nakedness that made me turn and run. That look terrified me. I cannot remember how it was now - only that he was very bad and I must run for my life. I think he started to follow me but I must have been too quick because I was soon back amongst the other children and the safety of the nuns and our three burly drivers. I think that was when I had my first full asthma attack, because I didn't have the breath to tell the nun in charge that year, Mother Mary Woolstan, about the naked man. I was settled down to rest on the back seats of the *charabanc* and suppose I must have slept because that is really all I remember of the 1939 Spring picnic. That terrifying expression on the naked man's face – and, the asthma attack, put an end to my picnic enjoyment that year.

By the Spring of 1940, I was no longer so inclined to wander off on my own. The minute I stepped off the bus and smelt the flowers in the air, my chest began to tighten. This time I went for help at once and was given smelling salts and made to sit down. Mother Mary Joan looked worried, maybe wondering whether bluebell woods, for all their beauty and being the work of an artistic God, might not be so good for small girls with an asthma problem. I sat quietly near her as she talked through the children's Nature tasks for the morning, and it was not my chest that was worrying me but the memory, never shared, of that nightmare man and the sickening look on his face. I made a good recovery, but stayed very close to the buses and the adults for the whole of the day.

5 - Summer at school, 1936 - hay-making for juniors (Dione circled top centre)

"I cannot believe how good Dione has been all day today," I heard Mother say to Sister Burkmanns on the way home that evening. "I don't think she is coming down with anything, and her chest settled quickly. She just seemed so docile - not like her at all." and they laughed quietly together. I loved those two. They were my favourite nuns and the depth of their patience where I was concerned seems to have been fathomless. The only doll I ever owned (I did not like dolls, preferring animals or things like Meccano sets for building things) was named Joan Burkmanns after them both. I won JB in a school raffle. She had silver teeth and a distinct glare of revolution in her bright blue glass eyes and tiny, pursed lips. The only reason I liked her at all was because of that look of impending disobedience all over her face. She was not going to do a thing I told her to do - and I absolutely understood her! We were friends in a limited way and only she and I knew why! Joan Burkmanns was to meet a tragic end from which some deep-down sense of loss remains as a sad echo.

It had been decided the previous September, at the beginning of the school year, that the Junior School was to do the play, *The Song of Hiawatha,* the long poetic saga by American poet H. W. Longfellow, for the end–of–year Prize-giving on the last day of the 1940 Summer term and that I, taking the part of Minnehaha, was to sing the main solo - "Onaway, Awake Beloved." This meant a great deal of really hard work for all three terms because, of course, we made all our own stage sets, under the eagle eye of Art mistress Mother St. Edward (She eventually became *Reverend Mother*, as our Head Mistress was called). She was a consummate artist, of the modern school, so that things had to be created with great swathes of colour and simple outlines: *effect* was what it was all about. Her Art and style had a lasting influence on Junie, whose own artwork was becoming ever more innovative and showed tremendous talent. It was noted that Dione was quite good at Art too. In my own head it was English that came first, second and third - then Singing and then Art. I really did not want to play the piano, which Moo decided should be my musical instrument. I'd have loved to have played a wind instrument such as a clarinet, but they did not teach this in the Junior school, and Moo was quite firm on the subject, saying that clarinets were not played by Ladies, I didn't have enough 'puff' to spare for a wind instrument and, as I clearly had a natural ear for music, the piano was what I was going to flourish with. Anyway we had a piano in the London flat and it had to be used, and so that is what I was taught.

Singing was never a problem. I obviously enjoyed the sound of my own voice and adored the sensation of soaring like a bird when the moment was right, where the chords could be thrown through their octaves, drop to a whisper, float through glorious lilting melody. Singing, I came to recognise, was just like flying. It felt like a form of escape, though from what I had no idea at that time.

In our daily periods of 'free time', I loved to go down to the very end of The Laburnum Walk, south of the Junior School building, which ran along its southern boundary wall beside the upper Hastings road. On its other side a steep bank rose up into the great hay field where we romped and built hay nests every summer, with the school chapel overlooking it, thus enclosing the pathway like a softly embracing green tunnel.

6 - Mother Mary Damien, 1935 with Dione and Junie on her left

The Laburnum Walk was a place where the nuns, and sometimes the children, would go to say their rosary, to pray quietly, to contemplate. At the very end was an old fallen tree trunk in the undergrowth and I discovered how easy it was to climb into it, between two almost fossilised branches and sit in comfort to think my thoughts - and to sing to myself. I practiced my Minnehaha solo there daily for weeks on end, quite apart from the official song practice that all the singers did twice a week, then daily. As a result, my progress (which must surely have been heard now and then by the nuns), strength of vocal chords and depth of emotion in the part began to be noted by Mr. Savory, and the frown that he had originally bestowed upon this fidgety, often willful pupil slowly relaxed into quiet approval and even positive enjoyment. By the time *The Song of Hiawatha* was performed at the end of the Summer term, Mr. Savory had a glint in his eye; he had consulted with Mother Mary Damien, Junior School Head, and my parents, and he had begun to single me out for ten minutes extra breathing lessons after rehearsals, to help with my wheezy moments.

"Mr. Savory thinks you've made great progress with your singing this term, and might even, later on, have a career in singing," Moo said to me one day during the holidays, "but I've told him that, because of your asthma, you should concentrate on your piano. Anyone can sing - but not anyone can play the piano. Anyway"- as she saw the mutiny mounting in my face, "Your asthma is too bad for you to be able to take, let alone pass, any singing exams." There was little point in telling her that I *wanted* to sing, I loved singing better than anything at that moment, and that I did not want to play the piano at all.

"Why must you always argue about everything you are asked to do?" Moo said wearily on the one occasion that I had been unwise enough to voice my objection. So I stumbled through my piano exams, passing them with indifferent marks - and once I left school I did not touch a piano again.

The Song of Hiawatha 1940 was the last performance that the Junior School gave before the War rolled in on us and changed our lives. The evacuation of British and Allied troops from Dunkirk in early June heralded the end of fighting in France, when Germany took over the whole of that vast country, and invasion now seemed a certainty. The nuns efforts to evacuate the school rather than close it down altogether came to a head and they found two houses in Torquay, as far West as they could get, and as far as possible from the looming Enemy who were now only twenty miles away from us across the Channel.

That Prize Day was such a milestone: the pre-performance nerves and excitement as the great school hall filled up with parents and visitors to enjoy the Junior School's presentation of Longfellow's dreamlike 'Red Indian' saga. Our stage sets were all in place and looked pretty professional. Not all the juniors were in the play, but they were all involved in some way, as were many of the Seniors, so there were busy comings and goings as some sixty children prepared to fill their war-stressed families with pride.

I was excited, not so much because of the play but because I was going to see Moo and Pa at long last and would be able to show them how their naughty daughter had improved this year. We had not seen them for the whole term. The fact that we would be driving home in Winnie, our 'smelly' Rover, rather than the Batch, only slightly dulled the sparkle of my joy at the thought of us all being together for the first time in so many months -

but first we had our Grand Performance, and the Senior school Orchestra was already settling into its places and tuning up.

There was the usual struggle with my unruly hair, which had to be tucked into a wig of long dark tresses, which I hated at first. Junie was the dark-haired member of our family, and I (with Moo) was the fair-haired one. It seemed all wrong to be wearing gleaming black hair, so near the colour of Junie's, but I had to admit, on reflection, that I rather liked the long-haired part, and practiced flicking it over a shoulder as I had seen some of the girls with long hair do, once they undid their plaits! I was not a bit nervous about the singing, only the fact that I had a bit of tightness in my chest and was worried in case it heralded an asthma attack. Sister Burkemanns must have seen me puffing a little, because she came up quietly beside me with a camphor pad for me to inhale. She said not a word but gave my shoulder a little squeeze. I felt very safe then. It would be all right. And I would show Moo, Pa, Junie and everyone that I had a singing voice well worth considering as a career.

The beautiful musical poem, verse by Longfellow and music by Samual Coleridge-Taylor was a resounding success. We all felt that we had really done our best and had not let the school down. At the end, we all stood together while the audience rose and clapped and cheered - and I searched the rows of faces for Moo and Pa - and they were not there, only Junie's anxious little face, pale as the moon, stared out at me from amongst the shadowy throng. The speeches droned through, the prizes were awarded, the audience clapped and waved and were proud of their children - and Moo and Pa were not there.

"Your Father was sent off on Duty," Mother Mary Joan said to me quietly, when the day was over and we returned to the peace of the Junior school. She reached across the desk in her office and patted my hand, understanding the brimming eyes, red nose and the tight buttoning of my mouth. "You know what important war work he is doing at the moment, and he is not even at home right now."

"But where is Moo?" I wailed. "She should be here, Mother, shouldn't she?" We eyed each other because I felt that she thought the same, and that she knew I did. She put both her hands over mine on her desktop and sat there, long thin fingers covering my twisting ones with their bitten fingernails, pressing down onto them to still their jerky misery.

"Don't fret." She said. "She is waiting for you at home. She has been so busy making very special plans for you and Junie and she has such a lot to tell you. Just be patient and you'll find that all will be well. I promise you that."

Her words seemed to hold out the possibility of interesting surprises in store - and *good* surprises were always to be enjoyed. Maybe things were not so bad, after all. A soft tap on her office door - and Junie appeared.

"There we are then, my dears." Mother said smiling her gentle Irish smile and standing up. "Have a few minutes together before supper and then you'll be on the Batch tomorrow - and home in no time." She gave me a little grin. "At least you won't be car-sick into your school hat this time." She knew me so well..........

We trailed down the hill to Warrier Square Station next morning with the school 'crocodile', and we had no idea at all that this was the last time we would be seeing St. Leonards as pupils.

CHAPTER TWO

Threat and Respite

At the outbreak of war, fearing the danger of potential enemy bombing in our cities, particularly docklands, the Government packed off some 1.5 million children and some elderly folk, with labels and suitcases to the country where they would at least be safe. The country did not suit many of the children; nor did the nervy, cheeky city children suit many of the bluff, hard-working country people who did not have the time or the inclination to be kind and understanding with grubby and sometimes rebellious children from the distant cities. Pa had asked his two sisters whether they would consider taking Junie and me as evacuees if there was another mass evacuation. Both sisters demurred, though Auntie Mimi Burke, who already had one daughter, our cousin Michal, two years older than me, said that she would take Junie if nothing else could be found for us, but only Junie. Luckily the emergency seemed to pass and the subject was not mentioned again for many months. This early evacuation fortunately did not last long because there were few attacks on our major cities and gradually nearly all the evacuees trickled back to their homes.

On the 7th September 1940 the onslaught described by German wireless news announcers as *Den Blitzkrieg* (the lightening war, quickly shortened in Britain to The Blitz) began - and in London the raids continued unrelentingly for the next fifty-seven days and nights. Within a week, the children and elderly of London and our major cities were once more packed into trains, labelled and dispatched to the safer countryside, and this time they stayed there until all hostilities had ceased.

Junie and I had returned to London from school that summer and discovered that Pa had been at home the previous week but was now away again, and Junie moped and trailed from room to room and would have sat all day at his desk, curled up in his old Australian Stockman's chair had Moo allowed her to, but Moo herself was in a strange mood. She rushed us round the shops, out to lunch with friends, over to the cousins in Kensington Square where she sat in a huddle with her brother's wife Marjorie, whispering and becoming tearful. "Is something the matter with Pa?" Asked Junie anxiously, noticing this odd behaviour and expecting the worst. Moo blew her nose. You could tell that she was 'pulling herself together for the sake of the children' as she gave her elder daughter a hug and even smiled across at me.

"No, nothing like that, Darling. He is busy helping to win the War, like everyone is. These are worrying times". They were, because the looming threat of Invasion was beginning to hang over the whole Country. A letter from Pa cheered her up and she told us gaily that he had arranged for us to spend three weeks of the summer holidays at a Country Club outside London, away from the spasmodic bombing which was already making us a little jumpy by then.

The holiday that Pa had arranged for us was at The Edgwarebury Country Club at Elstree, north of London in Hertfordshire. We went by train and taxi and the beauty of the lovely old Tudor mansion took our breaths away as it came into view. It was a large timbered and whitewashed rambling Elizabethan manor house built in the 1540s. There was a curving drive through spacious grounds that were built and arranged on the side of a hill so that the formal gardens were all terraced. It was beautiful. When we went through into the hall you could smell the perfume of hundreds of years of wood. Wood paneling, beautiful carved sweeping staircase, timbered ceilings – a huge fireplace where great logs would burn in winter. We were welcomed by the family who managed the Club at that time and it looked as though they were having a whale of a time.

Edgwarebury could not help but be absolutely buzzing because it was not only close to three RAF stations but was also only a mile from the Elstree Film studios. This meant that there was a constant flow of film and theatre people coming for drinks, lunch or dinner, to meet potential producers, sign up musicians, artists and singers, and on top of that it was obviously becoming the unofficial officers mess for those nearby RAF airfields where they could get away from the disciplines of service life for a few hours to eat, drink – and be very merry. I do not, for one moment, think that Pa realised what an 'emotional' place he was sending his innocent wife and two young daughters to. The whole place oozed 'living for the moment' and even I became aware that there was an odd kind of excitement there. We saw so many famous faces and Moo would come upstairs sometimes after Junie and I had gone to bed, looking very pink-cheeked and flustered, and wearing that 'look' that she assumed when someone was flirting with her.

"I bet some man has made an improper suggestion to her." Junie would murmur. I was not sure what an improper suggestion was at that age, but by the time we left Edgwarebury at the end of our holiday, I certainly did!

I cannot really remember how Junie occupied herself during those three weeks, although I feel sure that she and Moo were constant companions. They went into 'town' to potter in the shops with the daughter of the household Pamela. They were also invited several times to visit the Elstree Film Studios which had just closed (and would remain that way until several years after the war) but the sets had not yet been dismantled, the offices were still in full use, and the place was apparently fascinating to visit. I did not go with Moo and Junie for some reason. I think I must have been more interested in Edgwarebury itself, because I can remember stuffing my skirt into my navy-blue school knickers and spending several days helping a small group of people to clean the out-door swimming pool. Maybe at ten years of age the glamour of the film world had not yet sunk in!

I loved the terraced garden at Edgwarebury and explored it, day after day, even finding a remote place for me to sing when I felt like it. This place was on the lowest level of the garden terraces, behind an old conservatory whose glass walls were cracked and broken from one end to the other but where I felt happily cut off from civilization and could lift my voice and soar up and away to my heart's content. What I did not realise was that although I was far away from the long-paved sun terrace on the house's south side, I was, because of the slope, just below it and my voice carried straight up to where people would sit and read, chat and drink.

One day, when I was having a stab at a new popular song that the band was playing in the evenings called "Ma. He's Making Eyes at Me" (a secret rendering since Moo thought I only sang hymns and had previously been examining the counterpoint possibilities for Gounod's Ave Maria) I had a terrible shock when I noticed the pianist from the band, sitting on the edge of the terrace immediately above me. I must have gaped at him, and would certainly have flushed as bright as a Belisha Beacon, thoroughly shocked, but he smiled comfortably and said "please go on. You've got a nice voice and it's shaping up really well. This is a great place for practice too". Well, I was far too embarrassed to continue and felt tears of consternation forming.

The details of that conversation have faded so that I only remember the shock of being discovered by a stranger, even if he was not telling me off. I do remember that he talked to me for some time and that I even sang something with him, and eventually he asked if I would go up to the house to have a chat with his band leader, who had also heard me. He explained that my voice had been filtering up to the Bar terrace and I had been entertaining everyone for a week. I was absolutely mortified at first, but was eventually persuaded to return to the top terrace with him and we went into the ballroom where the band played every evening. As I write, I am trying to remember his name. I think it might have been Nat Allen. I was eventually persuaded to sing *Ma, He's Making Eyes at Me*, and also another one that was very popular at that time – *Mama, May I Go Out Dancing'* which I sang (eventually with huge enjoyment) with the female clarinet player – again her name has gone but I have a faint memory of someone called Katie or Kathy Stobart, so that might have been her. She played a wind instrument in the band but for that particular song she was the other half of the duet, which went something like this:

> *Mama, may I go out dancing? Yes, my darling daughter.*
> *Mama, may I try romancing, Yes my darling daughter.*
> What if there's a moon, Mama darling, and it's *shining on the water?*
> *Mama, must I keep on dancing? YES, my darling daughter.*
> *And so on….*

There was an introductory verse which I can't remember, but I'll never forget the words of that song and the other one I sang that evening, *Ma, He's Making Eyes at Me!* Oh dear, it all sounds so trivial now, but at that time, when there was such tension all around, fear and grim determination in everyone in what was then still called Great Britain, that a little girl singing innocent 'naughty' songs made everyone smile. I seem to remember that everyone did smile that evening too, apart from Moo who, after I'd finished, beckoned me off the raised dais with the band, frog-marched me out of the dining room as everyone was starting to dance and said very firmly that there would be no more singing with the band, and I was to go to bed at once. I was much too young (which I was) and she was disgusted with Nat Allen's choice of music for me. I can remember Junie protesting that they were hardly likely to want me to sing *Jesu, Joy of Man's Desiring*. People were enjoying the jazz element of the band and the audience had loved my innocent little 'moment' before the dancing started. I was sent to bed at 8.30pm every evening after that and I never sang in the garden again, but one thing remains here in my head. Moo had tears in her eyes when she grabbed my hand and detached me from my new friends in the band. I would not have known what that sadness was for at the time, but in retrospect I guess that it was because she knew that we were all to be parted so soon after this holiday, and that is why we were having such a marvelous treat at Edgwarebury.

Pa had an actor friend with whom he was working. His name was Leo Genn and he would make several appearances in my life, the first being when he suggested that Edgwarebury might be a good place for Moo to take us as it was close enough to London for Pa to be able to drive over when time permitted. He brought Pa to have dinner with us after a few days there, and I found him a kindly, warm man – sad because his wife Marguarite had not been able to be there too – but flatteringly attentive to Junie and even to me. Junie was really blossoming at this time and I feel that our three weeks at Edgwarebury, living amongst a whole throng of lively, famous people had a real impact on both of us, and being film and theatre folk, they were a little larger than life. It had an effect on me, showing me that I did have a legitimate reason for singing – and I'm sure that it had an even greater effect on Junie who danced the night away every night and had stars in her eyes for months afterwards.

She later admitted to having a tremendous passion for Richard Todd, who was one of the people trying to get bit parts at Elstree. He, like Leo, went into the Army after we met him at Elstree and both returned to acting after the war to resume their careers. He was a small man but nice-looking, and when Junie grew up, she always seemed attracted to men who were short and a lot older than her.

We first met Denholm Elliot at Edgwarebury. Denholm was a mercurial figure in those early days, full of fun and teasing which of course the ten-year-old Dione would have loved. He had just joined the RAF and was at nearby Hendon. Later in the War, when he was in Leonard Cheshire's squadron, he was shot down over the Channel and captured by the German Navy, lost a finger and spent the last year of the War in a prisoner-of-war camp. But all that was yet to come. I only mention it at this point so that you can understand what a long-term impact that holiday at Edgwarebury was to have on Junie and me. Denholm was to remain a friend for very many years after that, and might even have changed the way my life evolved, had he not been in Spain filming when my first marriage fell apart. But that is another story that we will not examine here.

Those three weeks seem to have flown by and it was not long before we were back in the Kensington Court flat and Pa had been away for several weeks. We were expecting his return at any time and a tingle of excitement always went through us before his arrival because we had a set routine that was always followed. He would ring the doorbell, giving the V for victory Morse code. Three short rings and one longer one.

Threat and Respite

We were beginning to experience nights of heavy bombing, which was actually the start of the terrible London Blitz. The targets had been mainly centred on the Docklands area where they could – and did – do most harm. Having brought comfy chairs and mattresses into the hall so that we could relax with all the doors closed every time the siren went, we cheered up to know that Pa was soon to be with us, because he could be such a fun father and when he was there, there was always plenty of laughter and story-telling, and all four of us would feel less worried about the nightly explosions and earth tremors.

The bombing was beginning to make us all jumpy through lack of sleep. The Borough of Kensington had been lucky up to that point, with only three buildings destroyed by random bombs. Most of the damage was aimed at the East End of London, and even though Earl's Court, Church Street and the far end of Kensington High Street had suffered direct hits, there was in our hearts that optimistic feeling that we would be lucky and most of leafy Kensington would be spared. To feel that we would also soon have Pa with us again made us feel even safer and Moo's rather terse mood quickly bloomed into happy expectation. She sang around the flat as she and Maisie prepared the dining table for lunch. The sound we were all waiting for happened at exactly the moment the air raid warning began its mournful cadence - the front doorbell ringing its special three short rings and a long one - V for Victory! Pa was back.

We had had so many welcomes and farewells with our Father that we had, without intention, fallen into a set welcome routine. He would open the door as we came hurtling down the hall, standing in the open doorway with his arms out, and Moo would be the first into them, followed by Junie – and Sally-dog and I made straight for his legs and wound ourselves round as much of him as we could reach. But this day was different. Pa opened the front door, came in, turned and closed it - so that our welcome collided with his back and then, as he turned to us Moo gasped and put her hands up to his face. He seemed to have aged twenty years. The right side of his face was blotched with bruising, his right eye was almost closed.

"Oh Skicken. What on earth has happened to you?" Moo said, shocked into using one of their private terms of endearment. You could tell that even smiling hurt him, but Pa kissed Moo with care and tenderness.

"Got into a bit of trouble last week." He said, standing in the warmth of his home, drinking in the familiarity of his surroundings and the love of his girls. He looked exhausted, our first view of him as an old man, and in a moment Moo had seen this and taken his case from him and the gas mask satchel from his shoulder. She shooed us away and, taking his arm, drew him into the drawing room, to his chair. He lowered himself carefully into its comfortable depths, closed his eyes for a moment and Moo said to us quietly. "Leave us alone for half an hour, and tell Maisie to delay lunch."

The door closed on us with a firm click and Junie sat down against it with her arms round her knees.

"Go and tell Maisie about Pa." She said to me. You could see that she was not going to leave that door until she was allowed back into the drawing room.

Pa revived and had something to eat on a tray. He was obviously aching all over because he moved slowly; his right arm had cuts across the hand and up the forearm, he dragged one leg when he walked - and his poor battered face looked ashen under the bruising. He had, he told us, fallen out of a tree! Moo tutted at this bit of nonsense but it turned out later that he really had, because - making a parachute jump into France, he had landed in a tree and fallen right through it.

However, at the time we saw him in this state, none of us had any idea of what he was doing. Moo told us all she knew after the war, when we were old enough to take the shock of realising how often we had nearly lost our father - and Moo her beloved Alan. On this occasion, Pa firmly rejected her determination to get the doctor to examine him for broken bones and internal damage. He had been seen by his Unit medical team on his arrival back in England and was simply suffering from external cuts and bruises, and physical exhaustion. He slept through the banshee wails of two air raid sirens that night, oblivious to the rumbles and earth tremors of the German assault on London's East End, and he did not even stir when a bomb blew up two houses in nearby Prince of Wales Terrace. I read later that there were 467 bombs dropped on the parish of Kensington during the fifty-seven nights of the London Blitz, and that was only one parish. History tells us that more than 40,000 people were killed in London alone during the Blitz and more than a million buildings destroyed.

It was not until the following day that Junie and I were told of our parents' plans to send us, by ship, across the Atlantic ocean to Pa's sister Iseult, who lived in Canada and where we would be safe from the imminence of the

invasion of the British Isles by Germany and the Axis
powers.

CHAPTER THREE

False Reprieve

At We were stunned; horrified at the thought of being parted from all that was familiar, all that was the essence of our very existence, of the possibility of something happening to Moo and Pa. Any amount of arguing and tears from Junie, anger and fear from me, was met with our parents' anguished determination to do the best for us, as other parents were doing for their children all over the country. Junie sobbed at Moo, but especially at Pa, and this was something that I had never seen her do before, so I kept quiet and listened because she was saying what I wanted to say, but she was saying it more coherently than I would have done. However hard Junie begged, the parents were unmoved, though. No, we were told, we could not go back to Switzerland because the War had blocked any way of getting there. No, we could not go and live in Scotland because we did not have contacts there who could be trusted to take good care of us. No, we could not stay here because we were about to be invaded, and this meant terrible times ahead; of fighting, death, starvation, of ill-treatment, and of some things that could not be discussed with such young females but which the parents could not bear to contemplate for us.

We were only allowed to take one trunk each and these had to be packed with practical clothing and the things we treasured most of our possessions. Our passages had already been booked and paid for, and we would be sailing from Liverpool, way up in the North Midlands of England where we had never been in our short lives. "WHEN?" wailed Junie, distraught at this final betrayal. Pa showed her a foolscap sheet of headed paper on which our future lives had been set out.

SS City of Benares, which belonged to the Ellerman Shipping Line, was due to depart from Liverpool in four short weeks on the 13th September 1940. She had been selected as an evacuee ship, as part of the Overseas Evacuation Scheme. There was room for 90 children on the passenger list and this small, elegant passenger ship was to be protected by sailing within a convoy of Royal Navy and Merchant ships. Junie and I were to be taken up to Liverpool on the 12th September and our trunks would go in advance on the 5th. We would, during the voyage, be in the care of a colleague of Pa's who was taking Secret documents over to Ottawa, Canada's capital.

Over the following few days, I packed my silver-toothed doll, Joan Burkmanns together with my black and white Panda nightdress case, thinking that at least they would afford me a joyful reunion and a reminder of home when they were unpacked in that cold and distant continent, north of America. Moo packed most of my things and bought me a new black Mason-Pearson bristle brush to cope with my mop of springy curly hair, no longer as golden as it been in early childhood.

"I'll keep the old one when you've gone." She said to me, a pensive look on her sad face. "It will remind me of the battles we have every day with your hair." She stroked my head. "It's such lovely hair. I just wish we could ever *do* anything with it." She gave my behind a little pat. "You will try and be a good girl with Auntie Iseult, won't you, Darling? Just for us? And you will look after Junie, Dookie? She's always so dreamy - just like Pa - and you know what a responsibility he is." We looked at each other - and I felt grown-up and very responsible, and at least a foot taller, for here was Moo actually asking ME to look after Junie! My chest swelled with pride and I felt the heavy weight of such trust fall about my shoulders. Goodness knows what I said, but I know that I determined in that moment, at the age of nearly ten years, to stop being a pain in her neck, and to become someone my parents and my sister could depend upon. It didn't last, but I did try.

We had a week to complete our packing; a week in which the nightly bombing raids seems to become more concentrated. There was a light gun emplacement in Kensington Gardens which we could hear every night, rattling away at the invisible foe, and the sound of its rapid fire was a 'quack, quack, quack' so we nicknamed it Donald Duck - and then, before the whole thing had had time to really sink in, our two trunks, bristling with labels, were taken away by Carter Patterson, transferred to Liverpool and into the bowels of the SS *City of Benares*. It would have been nice to have found out why that vessel had been given such a name but I was too miserable then to follow my usual trains of thought and discovery with my constant 'what…' and 'where…' and 'why…' that I was always bombarding Moo and Junie with.

Junie, head down and misery emanating from every pore, busied herself with the contents of her trunk, but was even more glued to Pa's side whenever he was at home. This last week had been good because he had only had one evening away from us. We said goodbye to our luggage and afterwards felt that a vital part of us had already left the flat in Kensington Court - and I wanted to have Joan Burkmanns with me for the very first time, actually wanted to cuddle her, as most small girls do with their dolls - and which I had always viewed with complete distain. Now I felt that I had lost my rock, and even understood in my child's way, the agony that our parents were going through because that is how I was feeling, having Joan Burkmanns torn from my side. I dare say I was better behaved in that week than the parents had ever known, because Moo was really quite affectionate and I basked in this warm glow, happy just then to live from one moment to the next!

The last day should have been one that I remember well, as I seem to recall other important dates so clearly but I do not have a single image to share. The only thing that comes to mind is the way the parents came and knelt with us as we said our prayers by our beds in the comparative safety of the hall, and we prayed to be brought back together very soon. I must have gone to sleep quite quickly, once we'd settled down, because the next thing I knew, it was very early morning and I was being shaken gently by Pa. PA! He was never around first thing in the morning when he was at home.

"Come to the drawing-room, Dooks," he said softly. "There's been a change of plan." Junie's startled face peered over his shoulder at me as I jumped out of bed, and we padded barefoot along the hall, still in our pyjamas. Somewhere, far away, a bomb exploded and the flat gave a weary shudder.

We had used the Kensington tube station air raid shelter now and then but mostly we slept in the hall when a raid was on. How strange to still be attacking London in the first light of day. The bombers had usually slunk home by then. It was probably a delayed-action explosion. The long dark hall seemed full of mourning, even in the grey half-light of dawn.

Moo was sitting on the sofa in the drawing room, white-faced with tiredness, her lovely fine golden hair in disarray, out of its usual careful coiffeur. She and Pa were still in their day clothes and it was clear that they had not been to bed at all.

"We have decided that we cannot live without you." Pa said, arms round Junie, burying his face in her hair. "Whatever is to become of us all, we want it to be together. We'll feel stronger that way."

We couldn't believe it. Our joy knew no bounds. We were not to be banished across a vast ocean to a strange land, to live in the care of a totally unknown woman, even if she was our aunt. We were to stay as a family, come what may. Oh Joy... Oh the relief.

The rest of the dawn was spent curled up in the drawing room with cups of cocoa, finally dropping back to sleep where we were - and waking later to find that Pa had already left for the day and Moo was in their bedroom, brushing her hair. Maisie, when she arrived, wept with happiness for us and the whole of that day went by in a whirl of pure relief. Within a couple of days Moo discovered that they had not been able to retrieve our trunks as they had already been stowed in the ship's hold - and so away they went to Canada, and two other children, who had been on the reserve passenger list, were called up to take our places. My invisible companion Ian, a constant private presence, was the only 'play' company left, and 'at least', we said to each other,' no one can ever separate us, whatever happens.'

There was a long fierce and more localised bombardment that night which sent us hurrying to the Kensington Underground shelter to join the throng of humanity that every evening lined the platforms on several levels. Listening to the dull thuds of falling buildings above our heads and feeling the whole tunnel system trembling with every impact, we were convinced that the very next bomb would find us, and that we would, after all, have been safer on the high seas, escaping this terror. Pa and Moo, both haggard through lack of rest, began to look agonised too, no doubt regretting the wisdom of their decision to keep us with them. The bombardment of the Capital was going to become more intense from the moment the Enemy set foot upon our shores.

The daily War News bulletins dribbled minimal information to the public on how German troops were gathering in vast numbers on the other side of the channel, preparing to invade. Moo decided that Junie should stay with the nuns, who had two houses in Torquay ready for 80 of their children to start a new school year a week late but in a safer environment. In no time, away she went with the Batch, this time to distant Torquay, with a very depleted number of children. I was to stay at home while negotiations with Auntie Dee, Pa's elder sister, were being thrashed out. "But why can't I go to Torquay with Junie?" I was aghast at the thought of staying in England but being as detached from them as I would have been in Canada, which was daily beginning to look by far the more interesting adventure after all. It was my health, Moo explained. They would not know how to cope with my asthma - and anyway, Dr. O'Brien had said that I had a 'murmuring heart' and must be kept quiet. I was most indignant – ME…. QUIET? I felt perfectly well, thank you, and I could by now manage my own asthma. Moo's recently unusually tender regard of me began to slip back into the old creased forehead and pursed lips expression.

"You, young lady, will do as you are told. " She snapped. "Not another word. We are doing our best for all of us, and at least we are all still in the same country." And, of course, they were doing their best. Moo must have been in despair, having to make all the arrangements for the three of us to be scattered around the South of England while Pa had gone away on duty again. I sulked, quite unable to see their reasoning of keeping us with them in England, and then for all four of us to be scattered round the countryside. Maybe that was their way of trying to ensure that at least some of us would survive the Invasion.

A week after we should have sailed away from England for our Canadian adventure, Pa came home with a bombshell. It is the only time I have ever seen him completely speechless, his rubbery, expressive face the colour of an old, stained attic sheet. The document he handed to Moo made her sway and, gasping, sit down hard on the nearest chair. Convoy OB-213 protecting the *SS City of Benares* had been attacked on the 18th September, and the ship had been torpedoed. She sank within 30 minutes. There were 105 survivors. Of the 90 children onboard, all but 13 were lost. The chances of Junie and me being amongst those survivors was probably very small. I shivered at the thought of what had happened to those children, overcome with the realization of them being flung, without any warning, into grey and freezing waters a lifetime away from land; alone in the salty element that swiftly snuffed out so many young lives before they had even begun to live. An hour after hearing of this tragedy it struck me with a

7 - SS City of Benares under sail (below) with scale model above photographed in the same building where Dione was a resident in 2023

terrible clarity that our withdrawal from the passenger list had probably sentenced two other children to death. Trying to sleep that night, another area of mourning dawned on me. My ugly glassy-eyed, silver-toothed Joan

Burkmanns had gone down with those children and I would never see her again. Her loss was my first experience of family death.

The tragic and unprecedented loss of seventy-seven innocent children hit the newspapers two days later. We were losing lives every night in every city by that time and the shock was strangely muted by the depressing news reports from the fighting front. However, the Battle of Britain was in full flood in the skies above our heads by then, and that alone seemed to be the only positive bit of reporting which gave us any hope. Those fierce aerial engagements to the death went on and on, and our young airmen leapt into their Spitfires as soon as the enemy appeared on their Radars, and off they went to clear the skies. It took them just over three months to win the battle of the air in 1940, but they did it, the final battle being on the 31st October. In that time the German Air Force lost 1,733 aircraft and the Royal Air Force and its Allies lost 915. It was the first decisive victory that the Allies achieved, and it had the most positive effect upon the morale of the people of Britain. Broad smiles appeared on the grey faces of those who hurried through our ruined city streets. People stopped and talked to each other instead of walking with heads down, shoulders bowed. The London Underground shelters became less crowded, even though occasional bombing raids continued and they were still to be in use as air raid shelters for the remainder of the War. The BBC broadcast more cheerful music, put together more humorous programmes, gave us greater words of encouragement and stirring patriotism. The absolutely inevitable German invasion began to seem just a shade less likely. "Thank God - oh Darling Girl," Pa said to Moo, "Thank

God you had that amazing feeling about keeping the children with us." He was gone again the next evening, and the mysterious name of Colonel Maurice Buckmaster came into the equation of Pa's life around this time. He had been sent, months before, to work with a new division which was called MI5 and had only now been able to tell Moo of this. It explained a great deal to her.

Moo was once more to be seen in the evenings, sitting alone in a pool of soft yellow light from one table lamp, mending something of mine or a piece of lace from one of her great table-cloths; a small round solitary figure, curiously bereft in her own company. We did not see Pa again for some time. Letters from Junie only came once a week but she seemed happy, and I always loved the little pictures she drew round the edges of the writing paper. They illustrated aspects of Torquay; the palm trees, the craggy cliffs of Anstey's Cove, the elegant hotels, and now and then an image of Junie herself. I missed her so much more than I had realised. I was still with Moo, and Auntie Dee was being difficult about having me.[2]

Homing in on the Underground was becoming commonplace to Moo and I and the anxiety of those first frightened rampages had given way to a familiar more orderly influx. The moving staircases would all be stopped and the tide of surprisingly cheerful people

---

[2] Dione was aware that there was bad blood between Alan and Auntie Dee but never knew the full extent of it. Brother and sister had been very close all their life (Auntie Dee's first book was dedicated to Alan) but that all changed in 1934 with the death of their mother, which caused a rift in the family that was never healed. That rift had consequences and made the 11-year-old Dione a prisoner of their enmity in Chapter 3. [GL]

would make their way downwards with little jostling, away from the open street and into the bowels of the earth to settle along platforms and winding corridors. There were several platforms but we always went to the Inner Circle because it was deeper than the District Line and Moo had some idea that the deeper we went, the greater were our chances of survival. I don't think she had given too much thought to the possibility of our means of escape being cut, should there be a hit on the upper station. The air in the lower confines was heavy and warm and laden with interesting odours; cigarettes, beer and heated bodies mixed gradually with the dusty air conditioning smell and a kind of sootiness which caught in the throat and was not at all pleasant until one became used to it. There were determinedly cheerful groups who sang part songs about 'rolling out the barrel 'and 'showing them the way to go home' - and those who played the fiddle or the mouth-organ, and there were others who played cards or sat quietly reading and talking or who just went to sleep. The toilets invariably became clogged within the first couple of hours, which was another reason why Moo placed us as far from the insidious odour of them as possible. There was noise and irritation and children running about and getting mislaid, but a certain discipline began to show after the first few nights and the wardens and WVS volunteers kept a freeway clear so that movement was possible to and from the toilets, their canteen and the main stairway.

There came a day when Moo and a friend took seven of us, two adults and five children, to the theatre to see *Where the Rainbow Ends,* a wonderful children's play where the children actually flew across the stage, several times – to my absolute envy. The sirens began their mournful wail during the performance but we were so riveted by what was happening on-stage that I don't recall anyone taking any notice at all, including the caste The buses were not operating on our route back home to Kensington High Street from Shaftsbury Avenue, so we walked as dusk became evening, shining our torches (we never went out at night without them) ahead of us in the dark unlit streets, huddling together when the drone of aircraft above us made us look for the nearest shelter entrance. "But we must do our best to get home." Moo and the other mother urged. And eventually we did – in time to pick up our pillows, small blankets and Sally-dog and make our way across the Square to the Kensington Underground shelter, to settle where we could in the heavy, murky safety of the Tube train passages. On this particular evening there was still faint glow of light in the sky when we streamed in with the human tide and made our way down to our usual places. Here and there a hand waved, a greeting was exchanged.

"Phew." Moo wrinkled her nose as we settled ourselves on our rugs and sat with our backs against the platform wall." What a nasty smell of hot feet. I hope we're not going to be here all night again. My clothes smelt of dirty bodies and cheap cigarettes when I hung them up this morning." But we were there all night - as we had been the previous night and the night before that. There was no trouble in our part of London for the first hour or two, the wardens reported but then the bombs got closer.

There was little sleep that night. The air was thick and dusty, and I had some trouble with breathing. There was movement all around as those trying to rest on the crowded platforms shifted, whispered and sometimes sang to each other, and many must have been wondering, as the explosions above us continued, whether this would be the night when they were made homeless. In the morning, when the All Clear sounded, everyone trailed wearily up the stationary escalators into the morning air, emerging in a thin straggle into another grey day. Moo stood in the road with her hand against her cheek, looking about her with growing dismay at crumbled buildings, gouts of dirty smoke pluming upwards into the pink sky, piles of rubble, a car almost flattened by a single great slab of concrete. Tired men and women shuffled mechanically between ambulances, fire engines, mobile water cisterns, exhaustion slowing their movements, doing their best to clear the road so that the emergency services could pass through. The air was suddenly filled with the chaotic noise of ambulance sirens, the swishing roar of the water hoses, a voice raised in pain, another in anger. Some distance away, the side of a building suddenly folded and collapsed as we watched, keeling over with a vibrating rumble that shook the earth under our feet, and disappearing in a billow of red brick dust.

We took our time, Moo, Sally-dog and me, hanging tightly onto each other and trying to avoid passing anything that looked as though it might collapse on us. Sally-dog cocked her leg on everything she could see, so that I had to pull her away from so much that was scent-worthy but dangerous. We made our way past the big department store, Derry and Toms, which had obviously suffered considerable damage from incendiary bombs and worse, doing our best to avoid the great shards of glass where the Store's huge display windows had been blown in, and turned down the side of the building along Derry Street, our usual short cut through

Kensington Square, back to our flat. Progress was a little better here, until we actually set foot in The Square – and found that many of the houses on the North side, backing onto Derry and Toms were in a terrible state with windows blown out across the central gardens and roofs and some fronts hanging open; dreadful gaping wounds. Many of the trees in the Square's gardens had had their tops blown across the road right down to their lower trunks, and the road in front of the damaged houses had disappeared under the rubble. Hardly daring to do so, we turned our heads in one fearful movement to the South-West corner of the Square – and mercifully Number 27 was still there and even had some glass in its front windows. Moo crossed herself, her lips moving silently - and we picked our way over glass and roofing slates, bricks and twisted guttering; along the west side of the Square, past Number 27 ('We'll go and see that they are all right later.' Moo promised), and then left along the south side, past the Convent of the Assumption and into little Thackery Street which connected The Square to Kensington Court where we lived. As the slight curve in the street opened ahead of us Moo stopped suddenly. The central block of late 19th century apartments seemed to have had all its windows blown away but the red brick structure stood strong and proud amid the remains of its framework of gardens. We moved forward cautiously, turning our heads to the left as Thackery Street met the pavements of Kensington Court, fearful of what we might see in our own corner – and there it was – the whole front of the house in which we had our home ripped open from the roof and top floor, down to our flat on the first floor.

We could see the drawing room with Grandfather Gedye's portrait toppled to one side but still hanging on the wall, Pa's comfy red velvet arm-chair on its side, rubble and dust negating the character of the room from familiar, comfortable home into an alien hellhole of destruction. Pa's study beside the drawing room was little more than a dumping place for all the blocks of ceiling plaster, joists and wooden floorboards from the floors above it. One solitary sad leg of what had been the family's precious stockman's chair poked up from a pile of crumbling brick.

That must have been a moment when both our worlds seemed to fall apart. How is it possible to explain the feeling of utter devastation in seeing the centre of our World as a family annihilated, our very identities destroyed beyond redemption before our eyes? It was almost too much to take in right away but with every second that passed another thought occurred – We had no clothes. Moo's lovely jewellery; things that had been family pieces and completely irreplaceable - gone. The good furniture left by Auntie Toddie - gone; her paintings, her Mother's beautiful paintings, all Pa's cabinets full of his inventions and the folios holding his and Junie's draughtman's designs…. gone.

Moo began to make small whimpering noises with her hand gripping my shoulder. "That was Pa's only capital." She whispered. "What will he say? What will we do?'

She stood shivering on a clear bit of pavement, eyes glued to the rubble, which contained everything of importance in her world. For some reason, and without any warning, I was suddenly very sick, throwing up as I turned away from her and aiming the vomit at a drain that was blocked with stuff that looked like filthy cotton wool. I felt frozen, rather than frightened, but all of me felt ice cold and shivery. Moo must have felt my tremors because she drew me against her side and, picking up a shivering Sally-dog, we just stood there until a man from of the fire brigade told us to move on.

"But that's my home," Moo said to him pointing at it. "I don't know what to do. Everything is in there. Everything." The man had simply been passing on his way with several other Air Raid wardens and clearance workers, with shovels over their shoulders and plaster dust giving their faces an unreal dead look. Now he stopped, seeing her distress.

"Sorry, Ma'am," He said. "Thought you was gawping. We'll be clearing the roads here for some time yet. You'll have to go and report your loss to the area ARP office, but best go and get a cuppa first from the Red Cross tea post over there. You look like you could do with one." He tousled my hair with a grimey hand and pointed to a tent that had been erected at the other end of the Court gardens. Moo put Sally-dog carefully down, dragged her eyes away from what had been our home and turned towards the Red Cross First Aid post, holding onto the collar of my snug green 'siren suit'. Sally-dog trailing after us on her lead, we went slowly over to where there were several uniformed people busy with tea urns and bandages. Tears streamed down Moo's face but she had no words, just that odd little animal whimper, like a dog that has hurt itself. I pulled Sally's lead closer to me and scratched the top of her woolly head, grateful to someone, somewhere that we had not left her in the flat, as we had done at the beginning of the Blitz.

I sat where the First Aid workers told us to go and wheezed quietly, with too many questions to ask and not enough breath to ask any of them, until Moo stood up and said. "Enough. We'll go and see if the Macaskies will have some ideas, and we can get a message to Pa from there." And that is what we did.

On our way back to the Square we saw Maisie coming towards us on her way to work and another day with the Finlays. Now she wore a look of great concern on her round face. She always wore a brown beret rammed down firmly between protruding ears, onto as much of her head as she could fit into it.

Oh thank goodness you are all right," she said as soon as she saw us. "I heard at the ticket office that there's been some terrible things happened here last night. Kensington Palace took a pounding. The trains are all late an-all."

"The flat's gone." Moo said to her. "Go and take a look. We're on our way to my cousins. Come and find us at No: 27. There'll be a lot to sort out."

Moo, visibly cheered by seeing Maisie, took my hand with a new determination and with Sally-dog picking her way daintily over broken glass and roof tiles at my side, we walked wordlessly back through Thackery Street to the Macaskie's house.

At least the cousins were all right, their house relatively unscathed. They gathered us in, ministered to our shock and desolation and somebody phoned Pa's Department. Most of that day is just a blur now. I know we were given breakfast, and probably lunch. Pa could not be reached but his department sent someone with train passes to wherever we wanted to go, and some addresses where we could perch until we found somewhere to live. I cannot remember real details of that period, hunt though I have through every corner of memory. I must have been switched to neutral. I did not even think at that time of what had been lost in the partially-collapsed building, having lost my most precious things to the Benares. Shock must have made an automaton of me, which is just as well because I don't think poor Moo could have coped with a whingeing child on top of everything else. I'm sure that we did not stay overnight at Kensington Square because the first clear memory of that day was, having left beloved Sally-dog with the cousins at Kensington Square, taking the train to Henley-on-Thames I have a feeling that in fact Maisie took Sally-dog to live with her, because they had always been great friends

CHAPTER FOUR

Free-fall

It would not have been easy to get from Kensington to
Paddington after a night of heavy bombing, then climb
onto a train at Paddington and off it again at Henley-on-
Thames. I was, it turned out, being taken to stay with
Pa's eldest sister, Auntie Dee, in Shiplake, who had at
last been persuaded to give me a home until the present
critical situation eased, and where Moo hoped there
would be no aerial dangers. Moo was to stay with the
Macaskies until she could find somewhere to live in the
London area; a bit further away from the docks and
industrial centre of the City, upon which the German
bombing was mostly centred. In the meantime, as soon
as I was settled she would be starting War work at the
Censorship, a building close to St. Paul's Cathedral,
which had so far miraculously escaped much damage,
even though most of the surrounding buildings had
been destroyed.

8 - Rambler Cottage with Auntie Dee (seated), with Guiny behind her, Cini on the right and the young Jenny in the front - 1940

I have been trying to remember the moment of being left on my own with the Buddicom family, but it has left no impression. My arrival at Rambler Cottage must have been quite inconvenient because Auntie Dee and husband Nors also still had living at home her two daughters, Jacintha and Guinever, known to us all as Cini and Guiny. So Rambler Cottage had to accommodate four adults as well as one small girl. Laura (Dee) and Nors had long since moved into separate bedrooms and although Rambler Cottage was quite a spacious and roomy bungalow, I ended up in a small store room that opened out of Auntie Dee's bedroom, a dark place that at first frightened me, and I was glad to have Ian's calming comfort in my head. There were two cupboards and piles of boxes in there, no window and just about enough space for a camp bed to be put up for me, with a little bedside cupboard next to it for my possessions, when I had any. I remember the air being heavy with mothball camphor and stale, overnight air from the Aunt's bedroom next door. It was a small dark airless cave, only accessed through Auntie Dee's bedroom, but it was to be my only 'space' for the next eighteen months.

9 - Rambler Cottage, adjacent to the tennis Court...

Auntie Dee seemed friendly at first and quite interested in the fact that I was a keen reader and writer of funny little illustrated stories, mostly about animals. She was a 'proper' writer because she had had two books published, the first in 1898, when she was just twenty-one, the second an historical biography in 1935. By the early 1930s, Auntie Dee had begun to suffer from some kind of heart disease and had gradually become less and less active, finally taking to her bed by the time I arrived on the scene. She may have become bed-ridden but she was compiling a War Diary. Every day she read her way through half a dozen newspapers and cut out anything that looked interesting. She had already filled two box files with these cuttings so that when I came to Rambler Cottage, it very soon became my daily job to carefully cut from the printed pages, the articles she indicated with a pencil. I do not know what happened to all her 'diary notes' because no book evolved from them. I privately felt that it was cheating to cut out other peoples' reports and not to do the writing herself, but I dare say she was not well enough to tackle the discipline of serious writing by then. Auntie Dee had a very sharp tongue and gave orders in a most imperious way so that I quickly felt that my place was a distinctly servile one. To describe the way I fitted into the household you would say that I became the 'tweeny', which Great Houses had in days gone by – the little 'in-between maid' whose duties were between the kitchen staff and the House staff!

One thing I found interesting at Rambler Cottage was the collection of paintings lining every inch of the walls. They had originally adorned the much more spacious walls of the neighbouring Quarry House, and before that, many of them had been in the London home of Great

10 - ...Quarry House on the adjacent edge of the tennis court to Rambler Cottage

Grandfather Gedye until his death. The painting that

always fascinated me most was, by then, in the drawing room at Rambler Cottage. It was one of a pair of large marine oil paintings of waves with fishing boats and the distant coast of Cornwall in the background and had, with its companion seascape, been painted on commission for Grandfather Gedye by a well-known marine painter called David James in 1888. The one I liked best of that pair had a particularly attractive long rolling wave, exquisitely painted right across the width of the canvas, and there were two areas that I became quite dreamy about. I tended to go and hide inside one part of that wave when Auntie Dee had been telling me off for some misdeed, but at the other end of the same wave there was a section that looked like a lovely hammock and I would in my imagination go and lie in it and be rocked by the gentle movement of the current, until I was brought sharply back to earth by Auntie Dee snapping at me to stop day-dreaming! When I mentioned this to Pa one day he laughed and said that when he was a small boy, he too had 'hidden' in the same water-cave now and then.

11 - Cini - 1948

The most immediately interesting member of this new family was Jacintha, Auntie Dee's elder daughter, who must have been about 40 by then. She was very petite and wore size 3 shoes, only half a size larger than my own. She was elegantly dressed, her hair beautifully shaped and she wore only a trace of make-up on her face. She smoked Balkan Sobranies from a lovely long amber cigarette holder and also had a jet one for evening use. She was extremely intelligent and had as extensive a vocabulary as her mother, which they used on each other with some frequency, with and without barbs, although Jacintha (Cini) was genuinely devoted to her mother. Cini was a poet as well as a writer and moved in literary circles, which included many well-known writers, poets and artists of her period – Virginia Woolf and her sister Vanessa Bell being an example.

Auntie Dee's husband Nors was a tall, rangy, silent man with jet black hair going grey and a droopy 'pepper & salt' moustache. He had been very good looking as a young man and you could still see what had attracted Auntie Dee when he smiled, but he rarely opened his mouth unless it was to eat or to answer a question. Because Auntie Dee – and also Cini – were great talkers, debaters, arguers, his silence was not surprising, but he was in fact a kindly, gentle person and I never remember him being unkind or scolding me. Really he was very good to me, and so were Cini and Guiny – especially Guiny. We were both the youngest in our families and Guiny was extremely observant, even if she was a little like Nors in that she was tall and skinny with pulled-back straight dark hair and made no attempt to wear attractive feminine clothes. Her voice tended to be gruff, with an odd crack in it at times. She was always quiet in company, and only became animated when we were on our own, and she would tell me all about the magical history of the plants and creatures that lived in the garden. This immediately caught my imagination and I attached myself to her whenever she was home (she had volunteered to work in a munitions factory in Reading three days a week during the War).

Guiny was the car driver when Nors was out and she drove the old family Daimler to Henley for shopping, to Reading for her work, and by the time I was eleven, she had started to teach me to drive – up and down the Fair Mile at Henley which was an absolutely straight road up an incline. I would sit on her lap and steer, and she would manage the foot brakes and clutch because my legs were too short to reach them, and I would change gear with her hand firmly guiding mine so that I didn't 'crash' them. This was a tremendous excitement – especially as it was a secret, not to be shared with anyone else in the family or we would be stopped. Children have good instincts and all my instincts concerning Guiny were relaxed and affectionate, and very grateful indeed for her company and friendship. She looked after me with practical rather than affectionate attention, quite deliberately often shielding me from her mother's growing game of 'Dione-baiting'.

One of my household duties was to bring in the eggs each day from the henhouse where Guiny kept a dozen or more chickens of various colours and sizes. I learned to clean the coops out daily; to give the hens fresh nesting straw and pellets; and Guiny showed me how she preserved some of the largest eggs in a huge carboy filled with a liquid called Waterglass. This liquid was

12 - Guiny, 1926

more in use then than the favoured Isinglass, a special preparation for preserving things, and which became

impossible to get once War had cut off supplies from Scandinavia. Waterglass is, I'm told, a sodium silicate solution, used for 'sealing' egg shells, thereby preserving the eggs inside. It seems to have worked very well because I am almost certain that all country people did this in those days and it was, in wartime, especially useful during the increasing food shortages.

Working with Guiny was my favourite occupation because it kept me out of the house and away from Auntie Dee's beady eyes which, as the weeks turned into months, seemed to be fixed on me with an expression that I could not quite fathom, but which made me feel really uncomfortable. Because I was beginning to create a life of my own inside my head so that I would not feel as lonely as this solitary existence made me, she seemed to think that I was hiding something and was constantly making me turn out my pockets. She never found anything more criminal than an occasional stale crust to give to the hedgehogs, until Guiny told me that bread was not good for them.

Afte a time, I was also required to hand over my precious current exercise book so that Auntie Dee could check to see if I was writing any spurious complaints about her or her family. I think the reason for this must have originated from the letter I wrote Moo a couple of weeks after I'd arrived at Rambler Cottage, in which I begged her to come and take me back with her because I was so unhappy. Maybe I did not explain why I was not happy, and certainly did not make nasty remarks about any of the Norsworthy/Buddicoms, because the reason for my unhappiness was simply that I had once more been banished from my home to live amongst strangers, much as I had done when I was three – and I still wanted, more than anything on earth, just to live my life close to Moo – and to Junie and Pa when they were around. But Auntie Dee must have steamed open the letter that Nors had offered to post for me, had read of my homesickness and thought what an ungrateful little brat I was when they had virtually scraped me off the London streets!

I eventually settled down to the very different daily routine of life in Shiplake, and that distant but gloriously happy three weeks of colour and music at Edgwarebury, which was my only haven of happiness then, faded into drab daily routine. I did not go to school but Auntie Dee gave me English, Arithmetic and History lessons every morning and I had two hours homework to do at some point during the rest of the day. She did not take long to give up on me on the subject of Arithmetic, but I must have made her feel more encouraged in English subjects because we seemed to spend more time on them than on anything else. I like to think that she was probably very good for my later grammar and punctuation!

The Quarry House estate had, five houses on it, with a patch of open ground in the middle where there were several trees with interesting shapes, into which I loved to climb. Uncle Dudie's house,[3] Bolney Trevor, was at the South end of the land, nearest to the fruit and veg' nurseries, the village shop, railway station and the river Thames. Quaint Cottage had been built between Bolney Trevor and Quarry House, both on the West side of the

---

[3] Uncle Dudie was Roy Finlay, Pa's brother, who founded and owned Phylis Court in Henley, which became the playground of the rich in London Society [DV]

property, Rambler Cottage was on the North side and the Thatched Cottage was to the East. The open land was filled with tall grasses and a central stand of about six trees. One tree in particular had a branch that draped itself over the wall of The Thatched Cottage and into its garden. I found I could climb quite high up this tree, and the overhanging branch had a comfortable angle which allowed me to sit with my back to the main trunk and my legs stretched out along the branch, invisible amongst the leafy boughs in summer, and fascinated by the events unfolding over the wall.

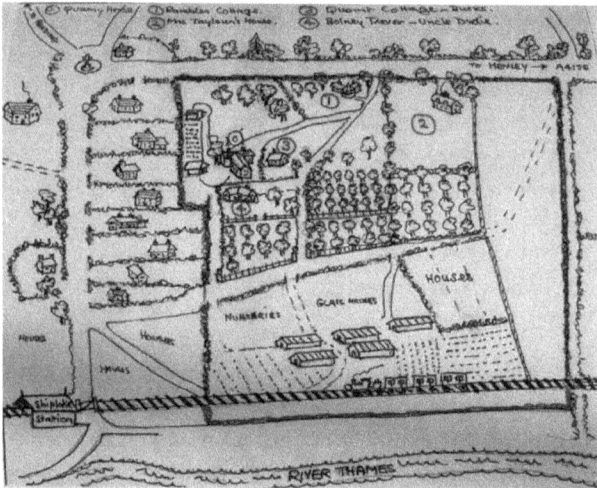

13 - Map of Finlay Estate in Shiplake, 1942

A very strange woman of indeterminate age, Mrs Taylour, lived in The Thatched Cottage and could be seen worshipping the sunset whenever there was one – and probably the sunrise too, had I been watching at that time. Having taken a long lease on the Thatched Cottage, Mrs Taylour tried to get the house name changed to Lavendar Cottage, which Auntie Dee always refused as no one was going to tell her what to call her property. So this strange woman, stout and adorned always with floaty scarves and long ropes of multi-coloured beads, began to plant lavender bushes all over the very pretty garden. One day I noticed that workmen were putting up several small buildings, which looked as though they would become garden sheds – but it gradually became clear that they were little houses. They looked like rather pretty little summer houses until Mrs Taylour appeared one afternoon, wheeling a pram. She would wheel the pram round and round the garden, singing to the baby tucked into its shawl and lace pram cover and I thought how happy she must be to have some company of her own at last as she had seemed as lonely as I was. It gradually became clear, as the little houses were completed and then painted, that they were nearly life-sized dolls houses, in which she could sit with her 'babies' - all of which turned out to be dolls. The three little houses were very simple in design but each painted a bright colour. There was a pink house, a blue house and white and yellow house. Each had a front door and one window beside it and I longed to discover what was inside but was never able to pluck up enough courage to invade the lavender garden and peer through the windows. In time, no less than nine dolls were added to Mrs Taylour's family, and sometimes in the summer she would bring them all out to have a marvelous tea party in the open doorway of one or other of the bright little houses. Watching her kept me busy for hours on end, so that Auntie Dee became suspicious and would not believe that I was doing as I was told, and staying within the boundaries of the Estate. I felt increasingly uncomfortable as her eyes seemed glued to me whenever I was within her sight. After a while, I actually began to feel guilty of some unknown crime. I have no idea what I felt guilty of – but the minute her eyes settled on me with that gimlet gaze, I would colour up and feel awkward, and probably looked deeply guilty of some heinous misdemeanor, because that is exactly the way her stare made me feel.

I saw Moo and Pa now and then, but not regularly because Moo did not like having to be with the Buddicoms on her own. Auntie Dee and Moo seemed to have nothing in common and I was aware that my aunt considered Moo to be a rather fluffy, empty-headed person. Unfortunately, whenever Pa did appear with Moo, he and Auntie Dee always ended the visit with a blazing row. In retrospect, I can imagine that it might well have been because Pa was not paying enough for my keep, but that did not occur to me for a long time and when it finally sank in, I wished it had not - because I ended up back on the street!

During the Spring of 1941, some new tenants moved into Quaint Cottage. Colonel and Mrs Busk's appearance caused rather a flutter with Auntie Dee and Jacintha because their constant visitors were Arthur

14 - Arthur Ransome

Ransome, a writer of childrens' books, and his glamourous if mysterious Russian wife Evgenia (Genia). The couple invariably came over to have a drink in the evenings with Auntie Dee and Nors, especially when Cini was home at the weekend. There was much animated conversation, with Guiny and Nors hovering with drinks and Smith's crisps, joining in now and then, but most of the time Auntie Dee held the floor unless Uncle Dudie joined them. When he was there he, Colonel Busk and Arthur Ransome, who was rather like a slender version of the Colonel Blimp school (you know, round face, piercing blue eyes under bushy brows and spectacles, and a bristly moustache that drooped on either side of his mouth) argued, sometimes quite heatedly, until they were stopped by Genia rising to her feet and deciding that it was time to go home.

The Busks and the Ransomes had, it appeared, lived on the Norfolk Broads and then at Pin Mill, Suffolk, where the two families sailed together, and the Busk children had featured in one of Ransome's grippingly exciting series of children's books, that famous *Swallows and Amazons* collection. *Secret Water* was dedicated to them. I gradually became friendly with the son, Michael Busk, in the holidays but he had just gone to Public school, I forget which one, and was therefore thirteen or fourteen – and I was only a tomboy of ten, going on eleven at first. He must have felt sorry for me, especially when the Busks realised that no effort had been made for me to attend even the local school, and Michael's elder sister Gillian, who must have been about sixteen, offered to give me lessons in the three Rs: Reading, wRiting and aRithmetic!

So, for three holidays, Gillian Busk gave me tutorials and Auntie Dee and Guiny set me various educational tasks during term time. This had the effect of polarising any previously learned education. I became a compulsive reader of books about people and historical events; Shakespeare and biography. I daily grew denser where anything to do with maths was concerned because, although I could see the logical passage and beauty of numeracy, I simply could not comprehend it – and still cannot. I was deemed to be a scatterbrain who could not be bothered to concentrate, and was therefore subject to on-going punishment. I did seem to have one unexpected friend though, as Arthur Ransome always made a point of having a chat with me when they were staying with the Busks.

"I really do not like children." He used to say – but then he wrote those marvellous stories about the Blacketts and the Walkers; the group of children who had such exciting adventures on Coniston Water that it fired the delight and imagination of not only my generation, immured as it was in War, death and destruction, but also of those generations who came after us.

Arthur Ransome was actually not at all gruff and prickly as some describe him. He was not affectionate in the way that Pa was, but on the other hand he watched and observed and he made a point of engaging me in conversation, encouraging me to express an opinion, guiding me in observation. Sometimes he would join Michael Busk and me in Quaint Cottage's empty garage where we laid out regiments of lead soldiers, and had great fun firing wooden matches out of the four canons, placed at strategic points. As you will appreciate, I did not seem to be occupied with the sort of pastimes that nearly eleven-year-old girls of my period were meant to be most interested in. Apart from Joan Burkmanns, drowned in the Atlantic Ocean, I distained dolls, preferring another of my treasures to have been lost at sea, my beloved black and white Panda nightdress case which Pa had bought me, back in 1937. This was when the attractive shape and colour of giant pandas, discovered in China a decade before, became a favourite childrens' toy all through the Western World. I loved things like Meccano sets because you could make such amazing buildings, cars, aeroplanes – *anything* with them, and it was great fun creating a crazy Eiffel tower, complete with stairs.

I suppose the things I came to cherish most in my small bag of treasures, were not only the books that Mr Ransome started to bring me when he was staying with the Busks, each one signed and dated with a brief but encouraging message, but also for my eleventh birthday the unexpected gift of a pale green hot water bottle cover which he had actually knitted himself. It was quite a plain peppermint green, apart from a small motif of Rupert Bear in the centre of one side. I cuddled this treasure every night for the next two winters but when I left Rambler Cottage I was not allowed to take either the bottle or the cover with me.

I suppose that Mr Ransome's gentle encouragement started to take effect because I had started to write some stories of my own in a school exercise book, which I always carried around with me in case I suddenly had a good thought to capture before it faded. After a short time, Cini became interested in my gradually evolving animal tales. I loved illustrating my stories and one in particular Cini seemed very taken with – the story of Edward Wigg, the hedgehog. Cini's sister Guiny, who looked after the garden, had shown me a little family of hedgehogs in the bushes at the end of the Rambler Cottage garden where she kept bees in three hives and I wrote a little story all about Edward and Mrs Wigg, and what they got up to.[4]

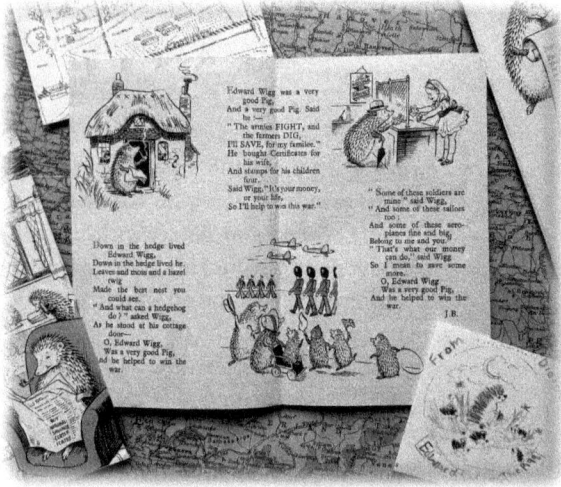

15 - Edward Wigg was a very good pigg

The day came when Cini asked if she could borrow one of my Edward Wigg illustrated stories. She took it to London with her and I sadly never saw it again. It was some time later that she gave me a little booklet to look at. "This is what we have designed for our children's campaign for National Savings," She told me. "Isn't it fun?". Well, it was fun, in a way, because it was all about

---

[4] I decided on the surname of Wigg because I started off calling the hedgehogs Porker, with reference to the 'hog' part of the hedgehog, but then it evolved into Pigwig – and from there to Ed-Wig and finally Edward Wigg. After that, Mrs Wigg had to be Polly because I saw her as a sort of Mrs Tiggy-Winkle who features in those famous Beatrix Potter books about Peter Rabbit and the rest of them. The Potter books would have been very much part of my childhood reading and so my inventions would certainly have been influenced by them. [DV]

my Edward Wigg – but at the bottom of the text I spied the initials of the creator, and they were JB. There was no sign of Dione Finlay or even DF anywhere. This rather took the pleasure out of seeing *my* Edward Wigg as the hero of National Savings instead of hiding, as my hedgehogs preferred to do, safely within the pages of my exercise book.

I looked forward to the occasional appearance of the other Michal in my life, my female cousin Michal Burke, who was two years older than me. She was fascinated by my tree viewing-point over the Thatched Cottage garden, its weird little houses and its even more weird owner Mrs Taylour, and we would sit for hours and chat up there – and now and then would plot to do something that I would never have dared to do on my own. One of those occasions was when Michal decided that we should go and visit Uncle Dudie. I would never have thought of doing that because he was not interested in children. Michal had heard her parents discussing our uncle and had come to the conclusion that there was something 'different' about him. On the occasion of our visit we knew Uncle Dudie was at home at Bolney Trevor, nursing some undisclosed ailment.

We rang the front door bell several times, but there was no answer so Michal headed round the side of the house to the back door and found that it was not locked. She turned the handle, opened the door and pushed me in, in front of her. I can remember feeling SO wicked – which was really exciting – and we crept

16 - Michal Burke, 1940

through the very tidy kitchen, out into the hall where we stood and listened for sounds. The house was utterly quiet, apart from the lazy tick of the grandfather clock at the other end of the hall. We peered through the open doorway to Uncle Dudie's study – no one there; no one in the tasteful drawing room and I moved in towards a comfortable-looking armchair, quite happy to sit and wait for him to appear, but Michal shook her head.

"Come on," she said. "We'll try upstairs."

We went up very slowly, and two of the stairs gave warning creaks as we put our weight on them. Michal was ahead of me by this time because I was feeling distinctly scared. I had just reached the top step with Michal in front of me when suddenly Uncle Dudie appeared out of one of the end bedroom doorways.

"What on earth are you doing here?" He asked, coming towards us. He was not very tall but seemed so at that

17 - Uncle Dudie, 1914

moment; clothed in a pair of elegant grey silk pyjamas and red slippers. Why do these images remain in the mind forever? I can see him now, his face pale and stern in the shadowy light of the first floor landing.

Michal was undisturbed.

"Oh hello, Uncle Dudie" She said brightly. "We heard you were not well so we thought we'd come and visit you to cheer you up." It was clear that we were not welcome at that time because there was movement from his bedroom, and somebody coughed. I cannot remember what was said after that, but we were told in no uncertain terms that if no one answers the front door-bell it is because they do not want to be disturbed, and coming in through the back door was tantamount to 'breaking-and-entering.'

We made our escape and I was so very glad that it had not been me that Uncle Dudie had told off or I would have been punished in one of Auntie Dee's many hurtful ways of applying discipline. All the same, he had telephoned Rambler Cottage by the time we returned there, breathless with running as hard as we could to erase the aura of disapproval that surrounded our departure from Bolney Trevor. Michal was mildly told-off, because both Dee and Prosper thought it was quite amusing and wished that we had managed to reach Uncle Dudie's bedroom door so that we might have seen who was with him. I think I must have been about eleven, getting on for twelve when that episode happened, because it was not long after that that I finally went too far and was banished forever from Rambler Cottage and the looming presence of Auntie Dee.

Shiplake was out of reach of the war or of no interest. The Battle of Britain had been won by the Royal Air Force and its wildly courageous young plane crews by the end of 1940, and 1941 saw virtually the entire World being dragged into the conflict when Japan attacked Pearl Harbour, causing The United States of America to go to War with them, and also join ranks with Britain and her Allies against the German onslaught. The Japanese began their advance down Malaya towards Singapore and took that Island on the 15th February, much to Britain's surprise as their defence guns were all facing out to sea – and the Japanese army poured down

85

through Malaya on bicycles! Britain also suffered terrible losses when, in July that year, the huge Allied Convoy PQ-17, in which my dear old friend David Williamson was serving, carrying vitally needed munitions from Iceland to the USSR, our allies at that time, limped into the Arctic port of Murmansk, having lost 24 of the 39 ships with which they had set out. The Allies were also engaged in North Africa with Germany's most famous military general, Field Marshal Rommel and his Afrika Korps. The strategist Churchill considered most suitable to deal with Rommel was our own Field Marshal Bernard Montgomery, better known as 'Monty'. Monty, for all his strutting and self-importance, actually did a great job with his regiments of determined British soldiers, and the German armies were defeated and removed from African soil by November of 1942. This monumental Victory did a great deal to lift the spirits of the British people at that time.

By the summer of 1942 I had settled into a routine for living at Shiplake isolated from the war outside. Although I was being taught at home during school term time, I still had morning lessons three times a week with Gillian Busk in the holidays. In retrospect, this was very good of Gillian because she was finishing her own education at the time, and studying for her School Certificate (this and Matriculation were the finals exams which were later replaced by GCSEs and A levels). Our very enjoyable lessons came to an end when she decided to join up. I cannot discover which of the services she chose, but because of the family's devotion to sailing, I would not be surprised to learn that it had been the WRNS. Her brother Michael 'outgrew' me and as I was approaching twelve, he became fifteen, and might well have felt a bit superior to be associating with a girl three-years his junior. So I saw less and less of him. This was a blow. I don't think I had developed a particular fancy for Michael because I really cannot remember what he even looked like, but he was the only non-adult that I was able to regularly associate with, and so he was a real loss.

I did my household tasks as well as I could and gradually became very bored indeed with the sort of subjects that Auntie Dee was 'teaching' me, because they ranged from essays on Shakespearian characters to reviews of what the papers were reporting. On the face of it, this was a good way to teach a child a wide spectrum of subjects and to expand the mind, and I quite enjoyed some aspects of it but I really hated having to report on what was in the daily papers because it reminded me of the outside World.

Somewhere out there were Moo and Junie and Pa, but the way things had turned out, I might just as well have gone to Canada for all I saw of them. In the eighteen months I was at Shiplake I saw Moo every few months or so when she came to take me out for the day and to bring me new shoes, or bits of clothing that I was needing as I must have been having a growth spurt around that time. When she came in the holidays she sometimes had Junie with her and this was always a wonderful moment because every time I saw her, Junie was becoming more beautiful, more kind, and best of all more loving.

Junie, I was happy to see, obviously could not get on with Auntie Dee at all, regarding her as a bully who dominated her household from her bed or the couch in her drawing room, and treating Nors as little better than a man-servant. It was clear that Auntie Dee disapproved of Junie too; mostly for her looks, muttering that she'd be in trouble the minute she left school the way she flaunted herself. This made me grit my teeth because the one thing Junie *never* did was flaunt herself. She did not need to. In fact, she was still quiet and dreamy and never made a noise, but would engage in calm debate with Nors and Cini who both seemed to be fond of her. Guiny said very little but saw that everyone had enough food, that the fire in winter was sufficiently stoked, and that Rose, who came daily on the bus from Henley and cleaned the house and did much of the cooking, was paid, that she had all the materials for her needs and that she caught the bus back to Henley when her working day was done. I only saw Pa twice in all that time, and the last time he came he had such a heated exchange with his sister that I thought I would surely be turned out of my little dark boxroom and put on the street there and then.

To this day I cannot tell you where Pa, Moo and Junie were living during those eighteen months. They did not seem to be together, of that I am sure, because Junie mentioned various holidays spent with school friends, and Moo continued to work at the Censorship in central London. That time is another black hole for me. Auntie Dee was always complaining about how much it cost her to have me staying at Rambler Cottage. Sometimes I heard Guiny remonstrating with her on this subject. I did my best to perform my house tasks well and I never asked for a second helping of anything because food was short for everyone. However, because I was a minor, the house benefitted by extra rations for me – which I never received, of course. Guiny would sometimes reward me with a boiled sweet for carrying a heavy load out to the dustbins or helping her with a particularly smelly or time-consuming job of mucking out the hen coop. I was so grateful as these were rare treats but it was around that time that I began to worry about how I could earn some money to help pay for my keep.

One day, in early summer when the cottage garden was looking at its colourful best, Guiny being such a good gardener, I hit on the idea of picking lots of flowers, tying them up into attractive posies and, with a few carrots and turnips from the vegetable garden, selling them at the side of the road, as one often saw gypsies and country women doing. Whatever was earned in this way could be given to Auntie Dee towards my upkeep and she would be pleased that I was aware of her generosity and was doing my best to make a contribution.

I pondered on this plan for several days and, as no other money-earning idea suggested itself, I began to think it really did seem to be a good one. I selected a useful vegetable crate and put it behind the garage so that it would not get used for something else. I did not dare to borrow any of the Buddicoms' table cloths but Rose offered to bring me one of hers from home when I told her that I was planning a flower stall. I think she imagined that I would be playing with my animals and pretending to do 'shops'. Rose was always a wonderful friend because sometimes she could see and hear the way Auntie Dee was with me, and it made her give little disapproving 'tststs' with her tongue against the roof of her mouth, which was always a sign that she did not agree with something. Very occasionally she would lend me her hanky to mop up tears that now and then leaked through my determination NOT to feel sorry for myself, and I was always allowed to scrape the bowl when cakes were being made – a treat that had no equal as our diets were by then becoming very short of sweet substances. She never managed to get my name right but I was always Miss Diney.

On this particular occasion, Rose also produced some fancy pink string for my posies and the following morning, when Cini had returned to London after the weekend and Guiny had gone off to Reading to her munitions factory – and Nors was over at The Thatched Cottage, sorting out some complaint of Mrs Taylour's, I borrowed the kitchen scissors and Guiny's largest flower basket and set about picking my stock of flowers and vegetables. Auntie Dee was, as always, lying on her 'day bed' in the drawing room which had a large bowed picture window looking right out onto the long sweep of the lawn, with Guiny's beautiful herbaceous border running down the left side towards the orchard and the bee hives.

I started at the far end of the long herbaceous border and, trying not to make unsightly gaps amongst the flowers, proceeded to pick and cut my way along the whole length of the flowerbed, which was certainly something like 20 or so yards in length. It never occurred to me that Auntie Dee might actually notice what I was doing – and it seemed that she did not because, by the time my basket was full and I had reached the end of the lawn close to the house, there had not been a murmur from her. Looking into the drawing room as I went past, I could see that she was asleep.

I took my flowers to the garage and laid them out carefully on the ground to divide them into colours and lengths and then, for at least an hour, I picked stocks and roses, delphiniums and even a couple of red-hot pokers, sweet peas and marguerites into fragrant and eye-catching little bunches, tied with Rose's pink string. I put each posy back into the wicker flower basket, arranging them so that they looked enticing and when they were all tied neatly, and the root vegetables wiped clean, I sat back on my heels and wished that I could have painted them, they were so fresh and beautiful. I sprinkled water over them, took the apple crate and Rose's tray cloth up to the main road (Rambler Cottage was built in a dip so that you could see little more than its roof from the road) and set them all up. I had about two hours before lunch time and was sure that this was the best time of day to attract the buying public. I settled down on the verge beside my flower stall and tried to catch the eye of passing traffic.

My first customer was the postman, returning on his bicycle from his morning delivery. He bought two posies at a penny each 'to surprise his mother'. "But I think you should charge tuppence," He said as he pedaled away, and so I put the price up and it seemed that this was a good idea because I sold several more posies within the hour. By the time the lunch hour loomed I only had four bunches of flowers left, when Nors suddenly appeared, walking home from sorting out Mrs Taylour's problems.

"What on earth are you doing out here?" He asked, taking in the situation at a glance, and eyeing the almost empty flower basket. I explained what I had decided to do and his face grew longer by the minute.

"You realise Auntie Dee is going to take a pretty poor view of this, don't you?"

"But it's for her," I said happily. "It's to help towards my keep."

He took the basket, scooped up the apple crate – tea cloth and all – and shooed me off the road and back down to the house. "Go and wash your hands." He said, "and then come and see Auntie Dee – and give me that money." I handed over the tobacco tin of pennies that I had collected and dared to say hopefully – " I'm sure she'll be pleased when she sees what we've got for the housekeeping." He grunted, pushing me into the house. "I don't think she'll be pleased at all." He said ominously, and I began to worry. I washed my face and hands, brushed my hair and put on my happiest face - but something inside was beginning to flutter and the feeling of the pleasure I would give my aunt had suddenly begun to fade.

I need not go into the details of that interview because it still upsets me over seventy years later. Auntie Dee was furious with me, accusing me of stealing the flowers from the garden for my own benefit; destroying Guiny's hard work, plotting to do unspeakable things. She had already telephoned Moo and told her to come down to Shiplake *immediately* to take her sly, thieving child out of her house, or else she would put me out on the street herself. She was, she said, utterly disgusted with me and never wanted to set eyes on me again.

With words I had never before heard ringing in my ears, I was banished to my boxroom and told to get my things together because Moo was coming to take me away. I could scarcely believe what was taking place. It was all happening at once – and simply because I had tried to GIVE Auntie Dee some money to thank her for giving me a home. Now she was accusing me of stealing - and that I had been going to put the money the posies made into my own pocket. I think there was something like two shillings in the tin – How could she think that way?

"I've had enough of you." She finally snarled when her vocabulary and energy ran out, puffy cheeks wobbling ominously. "Pack your things and stay in your room. The sooner your Mother gets here and takes you away, the better for all of us. Enough is enough."

I wept as I put my possessions together, the few clothes because I had arrived with nothing. I looked at the three books that Arthur Ransome had given me and wondered whether I would be allowed to remove the hot water bottle cover that he had knitted the year before for my birthday. It was in the kitchen but I dared not leave the boxroom as I had been told to stay there, on pain of death, until Moo arrived. An hour later, when my tears had become sniffles, I could still hear raised voices from the drawing room, and Guiny's gruff shouting, the crack in her voice making it seem that she was trembling. I had never heard her raise her voice before because of that odd crack in the vocal area and if she talked too loudly it broke, rather like a boy's voice that is becoming a man's. I sat on my bed, head in hands, miserably wondering what would happen to me, and listening to the different voices that filtered through my closed door. Auntie Dee, Nors, Guiny, Auntie Dee, Rose, more of Auntie Dee.

Eventually I curled up and must have gone to sleep because suddenly it was dark and Moo was standing in the doorway with the light behind her.

"Come on." She said curtly. "Pick up your things and give that box to me." She grabbed the box with the books and my best shoes in them, and elbowed me out of my cubbyhole, through Auntie Dee's bedroom with their stained green sheets, and down the hall to the kitchen. Rose and Nors were there. There was no sign of Guiny. Rose came forward and patted me on the arm.

"You and Mrs Finlay are going to stay the night with me," she said quietly.

There was a sniff from Moo and I saw that tears had been shed and more were to come.

Nors drove us over to Henley and all the while Moo muttered in her corner of the car, "What a woman…What a wicked, cruel woman." And I do not remember him excusing his wife, or trying to explain her reasons for banishing me in this way. I think maybe he did not say anything at all. What was there for him to say? He drove the old Daimler into the centre of Henley and turned left, coming to rest on Gravel Hill, and Rose opened the car door. Nors jumped out and helped Moo from her seat, murmured something in her ear, gave her a perfunctory peck on the cheek and slid back into the driver's seat.

"I'm so sorry about this Florence." He said, concern giving his voice a ringing sincerity. "You'll find someone to PG with, I'm sure." He glanced over at me and his eyebrows twitched in the way they did when he was about to make a joke." I know you were not stealing," He began to wind the window up, "But do try to *think* before you go making these gestures in future. You should have worked out the way your Aunt would view the picking of her best border flowers. And Guiny's vegetables." I hung close to Moo as the car moved off into the darkness and we were left, standing in a night-dimmed street that was cobbled and rose upwards, away from the main crossroads. Rose switched her torch on.

"Follow me," She said cheerfully, moving away from us. "It's getting colder by the second. I'll put the kettle on." She took a string bag from Moo and carried it with the box of books along a narrow path between invisible buildings, opened a gate and the shaft of light from her torch flowed forward to a porch with a doorway. She banged on the door with the corner of the wooden box and it opened, flooding the three of us with warm golden light. An elderly man peered out into the night at us, brow furrowed as he saw our three faces.

"I've brought Mrs Finlay and Miss Diney over to stay the night, Dad." Rose said as she stepped into the light, past her father. "Come on in now, Madam. What we all need is a nice hot cup of tea."

I know that we stayed the night in Rose's tiny cottage but no memories remain. Only sharing a feather bed with Moo and feeling deeply comforted to be able to snuggle up against her back, breathing in great lungsful of the loved familiar fragrance of Moo's *Attar of Roses*. We only spent that one night there in Rose's cottage, but no memory remains of her father or what was said that night. The next day we took the train to London, where

Moo had a tiny room in a tall, narrow house in the City, not far from her work. It was clear that we would have to find somewhere else to live but none of that has stayed with me. I seem to have blanked the whole misery of that time, post Shiplake. However, I do remember that I was sent to a new convent boarding school. Boarding school seems to have been Moo's answer to most problems and of course she was quite right when you think that the whole family had become fragmented by then, and she had no way of affording a flat or a house anywhere for us as Pa had virtually vanished. She had been in touch with the War Office and was receiving a regular monthly stipend from Pa's bank, but women were not allowed to set up legal agreements in those days and she needed his signature in order to be able to rent anywhere.

CHAPTER FIVE

Sweet Illusion

18 - Batchworth Heath House (left) in 2005 and right painted by Dione in 1977 from memory in 1943

While Moo searched for somewhere for us to live, I was sent to the Loretto convent at St. Albans, in Hertfordshire. I know that, by then, I must have been quite traumatised by the way my life was being fragmented, and am sure that I only had one term there because, during the next school holidays Moo joyfully brought us to Batchworth Heath House, which a distant relation of hers had agreed to loan us, free of charge as long as Moo agreed to be responsible for the upkeep of the house and the care of its valuable contents. Strange things happen during the emergencies of War, and the Bessemer-Wrights were flying to America in an American military airplane. Moo, suddenly animated and filled with plans, could not wait to take possession, especially as she was able to complete the paperwork without Pa's signature, in view of the family connection.

I must tell you about Batchworth Heath House because I feel that it was responsible for healing many of the mental and physical bumps and bruises that I had been gradually accumulating since the serene continuity of life before the War, and education in the calm safety of our convent school at St. Leonards had come to an end. Batchworth Heath House was a charming and elegant small Georgian gem, which I believe had been the Dower House for the nearby Grade 1 listed Stately Home Moor Park, by then, as now, an International golf club. Moo's idea was to make it our home for the period of the War, until we could return to Switzerland, and to fill it with paying guests who were following War occupations. There were any number of these people whose wives became homeless, due to the bombing or because of their continual change of postings. Of the stream of people who stayed with us in that lovely house (I remember many because they were nearly all interesting), a high percentage were working at Moor Park, whose main building had been commandeered at that time by the War Office (I understand that after our time at Batchworth Heath, much of the Invasion of Europe was planned at Moor Park).

There was Miss Margaret Barry who owned a very smart haute couture dress shop in Bond Street. She was a small, ginger-haired woman, with a plain but gauntly mobile face. She was always dressed impeccably in beautifully tailored suits, dresses and hats, and she taught both Junie and me a lot where dress sense is concerned. I suspect that it was through Miss Barry's interest in Junie, whose art skills were by then creating some very elegant fashion drawings, that Junie began to be interested in drawing models in dresses for the Autumn dress shows that were still, though goodness knows how or why, being held each year in London, despite the increasing lack of materials available and constant bombings. Everything was on ration by that time; food, milk, clothing and petrol. But Miss Barry, despite her concern for where the next bolt of cloth was coming from, was determined to keep going, as it was good for the morale of the population, both male and female. One small detail, I recall, was in direct contrast to her appearance. She had an alarming habit of passing wind – short sharp, evil-smelling machine-gun bursts, over which she seemed to have little control and so absolutely ignored! If you were unwise enough to catch her eye after such an outburst, she would look at you with ladylike disgust, as though it had been you who had just fired off such a malodorous salvo.

Then there was Major Hughes who was the agent and manager in the UK of that great Australian pianist, Eileen Joyce. Major Hughes, like us, had been bombed out of his London flat and decided to live close enough for daily travel but away from the danger zone of central London. Moo was delighted with him, because he was a great humourist and raconteur, and would sometimes after dinner sing in a fine baritone voice various songs of the day, including one or two rather risqué ones towards the end of the evening, when the wine had been flowing.

He was delighted with the house, Moo, and even Pa, who opened up to him because of his particular brand of mischievous humour and the fact Eileen was not only very beautiful but also Australian. Of course, Hughes quickly brought his protégée down to Batchworth Heath to meet Pa so that they could talk about Australia (she was often homesick) and this became a regular event.

Eileen Joyce, chestnut hair and green eyes, was a consummate pianist. It was a joy to listen to her because there was a baby grand piano in the spacious hall of the house, and on three occasions she gave an impromptu after-dinner concert for the household, much to everyone's delight. To my great joy, tinged with unusual nervousness, she actually persuaded me on one occasion, to sing to her accompaniment and, now that I remember this long-forgotten event, what an honour it must have been for me to sing to our Paying Guests (nicknamed Pigs), accompanied by arguably the most famous pianist in Britain at that time. I may not be right here, but I think Moo persuaded me to sing *One Day When We Were Young*, a charming popular song from the 1938 musical by MGM, *The Great Waltz*. It had been recently made popular again by that charismatic singer Richard Tauber who was, at the time, my idea of total singing heaven. For those who do not remember him, he sounded like Harry Secombe without the feeling of strain that Harry sometimes gave my own vocal chords when listening to him. Tauber had an effortless soaring voice and one feels that maybe the only person who sang better than him in that part of the 20th century was the great operatic tenor Enrico Caruso. Moo took me to see Richard Tauber on stage in London at some time during this period when he was appearing in *'Blossom Time'* At the Lyric Theatre, Hammersmith. Now I come to think of it, the song I sang might have been *My Heart and I*, which was a Tauber piece from that show. I know I only had this experience with Eileen Joyce once, though she wanted me to play a piano duet with her on another occasion, but because my heart was not in my piano, that was just too much and I backed away fast.

Then, of course, there was Bill Fox or William Fox, as he was billed in film caste lists, who was a real FILM STAR, and when he came to Batchworth Heath, he was in the Army but needed a place to stay close to London as he and his actress wife Patricia Hilliard had a home in the country, too far away from Bill's work. At the time he was with us (weekdays only) he was doing something between the film industry and the Government. His wife Patricia had given up her acting career to become a full-time mother in 1942, after the birth of their son. Bill was great fun and it was he who, after the War, persuaded Moo that she should let me go to The Central School with a music and drama career in mind.

There were many others who came and went, including Pa. The period we were at Batchworth Heath is probably the most stable time that the family had during the War and was a lot of fun and growing up for me. I felt that we were there for years but of course, we were not. It was more like a year or fifteen months. When one thinks about it, some of the people we met there were responsible for helping the careers of both Junie and me – so maybe it is 'meant' that we human beings should all contribute to each other in these small but important ways.

The first thing I did, after we'd settled into the house and Moo was organizing staff (daily help in the house, the garden – and a COOK, all difficult to come by at that time) was to go down with mumps![5] I had just returned from my first term at the next (the third) convent boarding school that Moo found for me. The Sacred Heart convent was certainly a happier place than my brief time at Loretto in St. Albans. The nuns were more friendly than those at Loretto, and the school had been evacuated from some danger point on the Essex coast to a commandeered 17th century Stately Home, Chilton House, owned by a family called Aubrey-Fletcher. They had a daughter, Karina, tall, slender and with short dark hair; a smiling, friendly girl, who spent some time with us in the convent, as her parents had moved into a smaller dower house nearby. The nuns constantly reminded us that we were in someone else's home and that we must be very careful of all the treasures that were still *in situ*. So we all tended to tiptoe round the place, careful of what we touched. Running in the house was strictly forbidden, as was tampering with any of the wallpapers. It was extremely pleasing to have beautiful things round us, and many of the girls had come from homes that would never normally have had anything to do with famous statuary, pictures, furniture and even pianos. How satisfying it must have been for the Aubrey-Fletcher family to feel that the ambience and influence of their home and its priceless contents

---

[5] Bringing mumps home with me, however, was not a good idea and poor Moo, up to her eyes in preparing BH House for paying guests; training staff and handling the cook with care, was difficult enough without having a sickly Dione laid out in her bedroom with constant need for Thermogene rubs, camphor inhalants, and looking like a large rabbit with too much lettuce in its cheek pouches! Pa started to call me Bunbun! [DV]

probably refined the lives and outlooks of so many of the children who spent their War there.

One day in the summer of 1942 the sun was blazing down on the lovely walled garden, Moo had two local ladies to tea to discuss something to do with the War Effort when Pa suddenly appeared round the side of the house with the large motor lawn mower. The lawn, which surrounded the house on two sides was L shaped and so he had not seen the tea table and chairs set out beside the open dining room French window. He came swinging round the corner of the lawn and missed the startled group by a few inches. He had removed his flannel trousers and put on a pair of Moo's voluminous pink silk knickers, which hung round his waist and trailed down to his knees! Certainly two of the five females hooted with laughter; Moo went scarlet with embarrassment but couldn't resist a giggle, and the two strange ladies were struck dumb with shock. There was not much he could do, so he gave them all a charming smile, and continued along the lawn, waving at them as he passed again, and then again. By the time he had finished, all five of us were laughing and gossiping as though we were old friends and Pa's reputation was enhanced locally as a charming prankster. Moo was pleased about that but wary of what he might do next. You never knew with him.

Regrettably, I was not to stay at Chilton for more than two terms. By the Spring of 1943 I was removed. Moo said that it was because of my heart murmur and that I must stay closer to home as the nuns did not want the responsibility of a child who was likely to have a heart attack. I do not recall feeling unwell, weak, or anything that might be a warning. I thought that I was in pretty good shape by then and beginning to settle and learn. It is more likely that the fees of the convent could not be afforded.

That year of 1943 was an eventful one for the rest of the World because, now that the USA had come into the War and joined the Allies against Germany and its Axis partners, things were beginning to look up. We had access to more troops now, more ships and aircraft, more armaments, more Summit meetings of heads of State to decide on strategy. Churchill met President Roosevelt in Casablanca on the North African coast, to discuss the way forward, the invasion of Italy and beyond. The RAF stepped up attacks on German industrial cities and 617 Squadron launched their extraordinary 'bouncing bombs' on three major Ruhr dams. They were forever after called the Dam-buster Squadron and cheered the UK population up tremendously with such an amazingly eccentric British invention as a 'bouncing bomb'. Just the sort of thing that Pa was capable of creating, only it was engineer inventor Barnes Wallis whose brain dreamed that one up. In September of that year Italy surrendered to the Allies after the battle of Salerno. Gradually Germany's partners were falling away and Adolf Hitler was becoming more extreme and arrogant; failings which would eventually cost him both the War and his life.

Junie and I spent the Easter holidays at Batchworth Heath House and, facing her last ever term at school, she was excited and had so many plans – most of which involved joining the WRNS, because the uniform looked as though it would suit her well. I blithely waved goodbye to my form mates at the end of the Spring term at Chilton, fully imagining that I would see them three weeks later, at the beginning of the Summer term, so I was very put out to be told that I was not going back. Instead, said Moo, I would go to school locally and be a 'Day Girl'. I had to admit that, from one angle, this sounded like a good move because I had recently been doing my best to be helpful and *not* to argue with Moo, and I knew that in this house I could be really useful to her – but what about my new friends at Chilton? School life had been serene and happy there and I was doing well with my three 'good' subjects. Feelings of mutiny and a return to that sad aura of disappointment caste a dark cloud over me, and the old horned and club-footed Dookie raised her head and, for a while, became a misery for all of us.

There came a moment when Bill Fox hooked his arm in mine one evening after dinner, and walked the now moody, no longer friendly Dione round the garden. He asked me about the things that interested me, applauded me on my singing, and seemed very keen to know the Dione who, by this time had, at nearly thirteen, become both shy with this intimate questioning, and yet eager to share my hopes and dreams. We walked round the garden until night had fallen and the first bats were swooping overhead, and he wormed out of me my utter grief at being moved to yet another school when I was just beginning to settle and feel that I had something to contribute. There were a few fierce tears which made me all the more embarrassed, and some gritting of teeth, but by the time a chill had begun to creep into the dusk and we went back inside, he had promised to have a chat with Moo and to try and open up the possibility of him recommending to the trustees of The Central School of Speech and Drama at the Royal Albert Hall my suitability to be admitted as a student at the end of my schooling, IF I knuckled down and really worked hard now. He balled his fist and gently touched my chin and grinned at me. He was not handsome but had a very attractive smile, which included his eyes. "Chin up," He said. "Your dear mother is putty in my hands." `nothing further was said.[6]

Moo found a place for me at the Northwood School for Girls, a 19th century secular day school in nearby Northwood which Moo felt would continue the type of instruction that I had been receiving at my various convents, even though it was an Anglican establishment. I had to wearily go through the tedious business of being fitted out with yet another 'used' uniform from the second-hand school outfitting store, trying to keep to the green and cream school colours. Moo managed a green school raincoat, blazer, tunic and several pairs of green over-pants because that is what we would be wearing for gym. "Goodness, gracious," She stuttered, scandalised. "They'll be stripping you naked next." And oh dear –YES – that is exactly what they did on the very first day of term when each class had to parade before the doctor and nurse, with only our pants on. Bare to the waist! I was mortified. I had never bared myself to anyone, and when I was little at St. Leonards they had even bathed us with a vest on! I stood with hunched shoulders in line with the other girls, few of whom

---

[6] In 1947, Moo did reluctantly agree to me becoming a student at The Central School, where I met my best of all Lifetime friends, Joan Williamson. I was only there for a term however, because Moo discovered that the boys dressing rooms and the girls dressing rooms had a communal wash-area and she thought that was just asking for trouble. She cancelled my place at the end of the first term, brooking no arguments, before I could risk getting myself into 'trouble' between the wash-basins! [DV]

seemed at all put out by this public display of our upper parts.[7]

"Hmm," said the girl in front of me, eyeing me thoughtfully. "Do you wear a bra yet?" I cringed and shook my head. What did I want to be trussed up for before I had to be? "Well, my mother says that if you support your breasts when they are first growing, they will keep their shape better after you've had babies." Bridget Forbes was tall and willowy and her breasts were mere pinpricks. She would not need to wear a bra for a long time yet. I had never thought of anything beyond the immediate future because life in my family was likely to change in a nano-second, from comfortable living to scraping the bottom of the barrel. It is possible to get used to this sort of precarious existence, but you never do deep inside, and simply become more and more insecure. "I'm never going to get married," I said to Bridget later, after the inspection was over. "Well, not until I have taken some sort of degree and have achieved something worth doing." I told her about Bill Fox's promise to Moo to recommend me to The Central School and she groaned with envy – and we became the best of friends.

Bridget and her parents lived in Moor Park, in the area that had been sold to build an estate road lined with large comfortable houses. They had a spacious and charming house in Aston's Road and I quickly discovered that this was only a ten-minute walk from the Heath. I made

---

[7] Having been brought up in a strict Roman Catholic household and schools, keeping ones' 'person' private was absolutely imperative but more of the secular schools made a point of disregarding what they called 'false modesty' and gradually I learned to strip down to my underpants without much embarrassment. [DV]

other friends at Northwood too. I have forgotten most of their names now but their faces pop up whenever I think of them - Pat and Gillian Lynne, Peta Rivkind, Beryl Basden. There seems to have been no trouble at all in making friends in this very different school, the first one where we were not shadowed by watchful protective nuns and, being a day school, we hopped on and off the bus and could nip into a sweetshop and look for things like sherbet and liquorice that were not yet included in our sweet rations.

My wretched chest was not my best friend. Not only was it ensuring that I could not do all the sporty things I longed to join in with, but it was sprouting by the day and becoming a real bosom. I began to hunch my shoulders. I did not want to grow into Moo's round soft person. Soft and round was lovely to have as a mother but I wanted to be sporty and slender, funny and tremendously popular – and how could I be that unless I had a shape that was approved by my friends? Some of the girls were quite cruel to the stouter girls and there was one who was nicknamed Skinny, and she was the fattest girl in the school. Whatever happened, I was not going to make Moo and Junie ashamed of me and call me names like that. My ambition was to compliment Junie's intelligence and beauty by being a good writer and a fun companion for company. That way, we would never step on each others' toes. Well, that was the way I tried to shape myself as the few talents I possessed began to shape me. It was therefore at St. Helen's that I began to blossom in every way. I found myself within a friendly, happy group of girls who seemed to accept me as I was, especially after there had been a singing test to find four girls for the end-of-year Show! I found I had something for them to value in me, and I relaxed and was entirely happy.

Moo soon filled her four bedrooms on the first floor of the house. She and Pa, Junie and I moved up to the top floor where we set up a sort of flat that left a space and bathroom for the living-in cook, and the maid. We also had Mrs Diaper who came in every morning at 6.30 to stoke the boiler, clean the grates, and scrub the front doorsteps etc. Her husband Mr Diaper was the gardener, together with their son who was what was then known as 'simple'. They lived in the lodge, which was beside the garage. Pa was a bit snooty about us being up on the top floor with the staff, but Moo had worked out that we could not make ends meet financially unless we had six paying guests. He suffered in silence and was especially charming to the cook, who was slightly nutty and eccentric but a very good all-round cook.

The term at Northwood sped through the summer months and in no time the holidays arrived, and with them a very grown-up Junie, sad and mopey at leaving the school she had been so happy with for the last nine years. She had shared such adventures with the nuns and the other girls, and when the Palace Hotel, Torquay was bombed, she had been one of the seniors allowed to go and help nurse the survivors. The Palace had been turned into a military hospital and other hotels commandeered for military training, and the Germans must have discovered this, for soon Torquay became a regular target for enemy raids. As you can imagine, it was not long before the nuns realised that they had chosen the wrong place for their children. They gathered them up and moved again – back in the direction of London to Hedsor Park, near Taplow, in Buckinghamshire, where they stayed for the remainder of the War. It is interesting to note that, had they stayed in their own school buildings at St. Leonards, they would not have suffered at all as the school remained un-targeted and un-damaged.

Junie lost no time in going off to stay with her friend Therese York, and later in the holidays, away again to stay with other friends. It suddenly was not as sad to see so little of a Junie who had gradually become a different person in the last two years. She was still bookish and dreamy but was now achingly beautiful, though still not fully aware of why heads turned in the street to stare after her, or of the power she would soon have over her admirers. Pa (and occasionally Moo) did a lot of socializing at the golf club end of Moor Park, and there Junie met Muriel Pavlow, a lovely young actress who looked as young as Junie but was actually at least five years older and engaged to another actor called Derek Farr. They had a cottage off Batchworth Heath because it was convenient for Denham Studios, only a few miles away in the Harefield direction. The fact that Muriel and Derek were not yet married but living together was not lost on Junie. Moo, of course, was very disapproving.

Moor Park seemed to be bristling with film and theatre people. Pa played a very good game of golf and joined as soon as he realised that the golf courses were still in operation, encouraging me, since Junie was not interested in sports, to do his caddying. Moor Park had three courses, one of which had been taken over by Rickmansworth Council and turned into the Municipal Course. The other two were called the High and the Long Course but we came to love the High Course because it had marvelously steep slopes, which turned out to be absolutely perfect for tobogganing and skiing in the winter. Because we had access to the Club at Moor Park, whose rooms were in the beautiful 17th century Palladian House, Junie and I sometimes had lunch there. The menu was very basic, the portions meagre but the company was interesting and there was always something going on amongst the members that kept us intrigued and attentive. We watched the beginning of a most passionate love affaire between two very well-known film stars; and seemed to be present as the whole sorry event blossomed, became ever more charged – and then exploded when one of the lovers' spouses discovered what was going on. Indeed "*lerv*", as Pa would call it, seemed to be very near the surface of everything, I was beginning to discover. I dare say that this was because everyone at the club was under sixty-five, most of them were involved with the War, and it was understood that many of them might not be there by this time tomorrow. That would certainly tip the balance if the love of your life might be taken from you at any moment. Living for the DAY became the way everyone lived then.[8]

Having been given the job of being Pa's caddy, which meant trailing round eighteen holes often twice a week,

---

[8] I remember a very attractive couple who had the most appropriate names I had ever come across – Mr Nice and Mrs Sweet. They clearly had partners elsewhere but would meet in the Club bar and drink with friends and hold hands and gaze into each other's eyes in a way that was becoming increasingly interesting to me, who was now approaching the first year of my teens. It was not long before gossip let it be known that Mr Nice and Mrs Sweet had taken a flat in Northwood over the top of a flower shop. Their visits to the Golf Club were not thereafter as frequent, unless they were playing golf, which they both did rather well. I wonder how that one ended? [DV]

carrying his heavy bag of clubs and gradually learning which club he would need for the next shot, meant that I had less time to be with my new school friends. Bridget Forbes lived nearby so this was not a problem but it was often easier for Beryl Basden and the others to come to Batchworth Heath House for tea than for me to hop on and off buses all over the area to visit them. Gradually, Bridget became my most constant companion, and she remained that way for quite a few years afterwards.

We were at Batchworth Heath when Junie finished her schooling. She was still six months short of the minimum age to join the WRNS, so Moo arranged for her to go and work for the daughter of one of her old school friends, Lady Hermione Cobbold. Moo had been extremely sociable between the wars, happily organizing endless 'events' in order to fund-raise for the homeless children of the World, or shell-shocked soldiers, or unmarried mothers. You name it, Moo loved nothing better than to be involved in it. Hermione Cobbold had been born into the Lytton family and lived in a beautiful home at Knebworth where later the very first Pop Festival was held. In those days of staff shortage though, the vast Knebworth House was almost closed down, apart from a wing that the family lived in, while all their men were away with their regiments etc. Junie went to look after the two Lytton children, Rosie and Harry Lytton and thoroughly enjoyed her six months with them. They were obviously fond of her too because they all remained in touch for years after Rosie and Harry grew up and became eminent people in other lives.

The day Junie's WRNS joining papers flopped down onto the doormat caused tremendous excitement in the household. I was so envious that she was about to go out into the wide world and mix with men and women from every walk of life, of every faith and every colour. Junie, being quite quiet by nature and not one to draw attention to herself, was noticeably nervous of this great leap out of her childhood's cocoon and Pa and Moo's fierce protection, but she was excited at the same time and the flawless pallor of her perfect complexion was unusually flushed the day we waved her off at Northwood station with Pa. He would see her across London to Queen Anne's Mansions, the WRNS Headquarters where she would pick up her joining papers and travel warrants before making for Victoria station to catch the Portsmouth train – and after that who knew what the WRNS had in store for her? I had to stay at home with Moo, who was worrying about the food bills that kept coming in, and the staff wages to be paid every week, and keeping the house and garden in good order which had been the one stipulation the Bessemer-Wrights insisted upon when they had left their lovely old house in Moo's charge.

In order to be able to give meat to her 'paying guests' extra to the tiny meat rations, Moo had bought several cages of rabbits who lived in hutches in the orchard and had to be fed and the hutches cleaned out daily. At the last count, there had been forty of them. Our family had always loved rabbits,[9] so when Moo said she was having

---

[9] Junie and I were quite fond of some of the rabbits. When we were at St. Leonards we had had a pet white rabbit (of course called Bunbun) whom Pa had persuaded the nuns to keep at the school in view of our frequent house moves. Bunbun had become the school hockey mascot and a strange

a whole lot of pregnant rabbits delivered, it never crossed my mind that we'd end up with forty. And as they all had to be fed – at least once a day, you'll never guess whose job it became to do this? Well, it was originally both Junie *and* me during the school holidays but, when Junie joined the WRNS and I became a day student at St. Helen's, there was only time for me to feed them every evening, come rain or come shine. Moo found a lad from the farm behind the house to come and do the morning clean-out and feed – but only during term time as he was another expense which we must save on, whenever we could. The rabbits had ordinary names like Max, Sloppy – and of course, all the names of the seven dwarfs in *Snow White*! They were born, grew from cute little bundles with bright eyes and twitchy noses, into large rabbits with sharp claws and often a strong kick. There was a period when they seemed to achieve a personality and to know me and look forward to my daily visits - and then one day that rabbit had gone and rabbit stew appeared at the dining table – and sometimes in a few weeks, things like a pair of rabbit fur gloves would appear in time for the winter, sometimes a fur neck muffler. It was never clear what Moo would

---

legend evolved around him. He was always invited to inspect when the two hockey teams lined up, and he would potter between the two lines, from one end to the other as part of the pre-match ceremony, and the side that he veered into the most, invariably and mysteriously won the game. If I had not seen him do this several times, I would never have believed it but that is what he did – he selected the winners ahead of the game! As a result, he was a very popular rabbit indeed and so indulged that he was rather the way that I had been with the nuns when very young and at the school for the first time – over- indulged and very spoilt as a result. Bunbun's end was probably through over-feeding but he was no more than four years old when the nuns sent round a sad little black-edged card to us all, relating the passing of pink-eyed and white-furred Bunbun. [DV]

think up next as the Country became more and more short of every kind of merchandise.

Medicines had become a problem by 1942 and so everyone in Britain was encouraged to grow things that could be used by the struggling pharmaceutical companies. The General Post Office put up a notice saying that the Ministry of Food wanted sacks of stinging nettles to be collected and they would pay 2/- (two shillings) per sack for them. Well, that sounded good to me as two shillings was a small fortune to us, and Bridget and I would comb the hedgerows, fields and woodlands around the Heath, picking nettles with gloves on so that we were not stung to death. This actually was a very pleasant occupation because, if I was on my own, I was able to think up a new story while I picked and stuffed. It was after all, only my hands that were doing any work and I began to work out detective stories with marvelously impossible themes, and the most unlikely of villains at the end of it. Bridget was great company and we always had more to talk about than there was time to give. She was an only child, tall, gawky and inward-turning, rather like Guiny, so I warmed to her right away. I could see the similarity between them, even though Bridget was emerging with a freckled prettiness that would stand her in good stead later on. Both Guiny and Bridget became different people when we were alone; more animated, more humorous and relaxed, so that you could see how good their brains were. Theirs were certainly a lot sharper than mine but I was more extrovert, usually able to override my own occasional shyness so that, being friendly and natural with them, they both responded and opened up. Looking back now on those growing-up years, was it possible that I had chosen these two shy women as my special friends because they were the opposite to Junie who was so beautiful, so intelligent and gifted; so sweet-natured and vulnerable – the opposite to my boisterous, argumentative self? Junie would never need my company, but Guiny did – and so, now and then, did Bridget Forbes.

19 – "Junie who was so beautiful, so intelligent and gifted" but vulnerable, 1947

CHAPTER SIX

The Fog Returns

It was late 1943 and the family was once more in trouble. Moo could not balance the books and was beginning to run up bills that could not be paid. That familiar look of stone-faced strain once more haunted her face, especially when she heard that Pa was to be sent to Bletchley Park, far away in North Buckinghamshire. The PGs were told we were leaving and very sadly had to find new accommodation. They had all enjoyed a very happy time at BH House as Moo was an excellent organiser and Pa, when he was around, a delightful raconteur, not to mention the interesting people who passed through, on their way to other wartime adventures. I had been so happy in that dear old house, spending hours fishing for tiddlers in the pond on the common outside the gate, and sometimes watching the antics of the customers of the Green Man pub the other side of the heath across the main road, who would on summer nights come singing over the Heath, fighting each other or making love, or all three! Moo was very disapproving of this side show but I loved sitting up at my bedroom window on the top floor where there was a perfect view of the whole area, watching the World go by and observing what was out there, waiting for me to grow up.

We began to pack our belongings, the staff disappeared very fast, and the family was left to its own devices. Junie went to Portsmouth; Pa went to Bletchley Park and then it was just Moo and me – and the Diapers who lived in the lodge, who refused to stop their duties because they said that they belonged to the Bessemer-Wrights anyway. This sort of kindness made Moo weep from frustration because the bills were too big for her to cope with. Her jewellery had been lost in the London Blitz so she had nothing left to sell, and so she had to turn to some of Pa's stocks and shares from his parents' Wills and fight to get his trustees to release funds for the highest bills.

I went to Aston's Road to say goodbye to Bridget, and we walked dismally over the High Course, back through the Park's tall wrought-iron entrance gates and onto the Heath, talking about anything but the parting ahead. I didn't ask Bridget into the house that day. Moo was in a distracted frame of mind, surrounded as she was by the chaos of putting all the furniture back in the places they had been in when we arrived. We hung about outside the entrance, by the pond, and when Bridget had said goodbye and started off across the heath I remember watching her figure getting smaller and smaller until she disappeared back through Moor Park's gates. I dare say I felt a sense of desolation at that moment because I was once again about to face the Unknown; once again removed from school, this time in the middle of term too; once again seeing my future as a vast impenetrable grey fog.

Pa took me on the train from Northwood to London and deposited me with the patient Macaskies in Kensington Square, and the next time I saw Moo the following week, she told me that we were to live in the Southern suburbs with a colleague of Pa's, a Colonel McGavin and his wife. They lived in a roomy house in Beckenham, in Kent, and already had two other PGs, but there was space for the Finlays – and so we returned to the South of London for the first time since my days at St. Leonards; to 38 (or was it 37?) The Avenue. What a distance I had traveled in those three short years. I had left the Convent, very much a child, and a spoilt, difficult little madam at that – and was returning to within fifty miles of Hastings as a teenager with my childhood memories taken from me by a torpedo, family memories destroyed by a bomb, had been made homeless, was ill-treated by family, attended three other schools, and was by this time having trouble working out who I was - and why. The one gift of I became aware of around then was the gift of optimism. It was the ability to find HOPE in most situations which must have come into play by this time. Turn a corner and find a nice clean empty space to embellish rather than sully. I feel that this approach must have been passed to me from Moo, who had had to find strength after strength to keep us all going with so little practical help from Pa. She gave me more than she realised, bless her. Now there was a new space to grow into.

38 The Avenue was not like any of the other homes that we had lived in. It was in a tree-lined, quite dense residential area but The Avenue had spacious

Edwardian houses on one side and the railway line on the other. This was not as noisy as it sounds because the whole railway line had been dug out of rising ground and so we had a bramble hedge and a steep bank, fifteen or twenty feet down to the track which did a lot to reduce the clatter and rumble of the trains thundering past. It also gave us a broader span of open sky opposite and the house was therefore light and airy and did not feel as suburban as Moo initially described it. There were two entrance gates to the house; one for driving in and the other for driving out, and a curved gravel space in front of the front door. The house was typical of the early 20th century Edwardian style, well built in red brick and plasterwork, with tall windows on either side of a gracious porch and front door. Inside, the dining room and study opened off a long wide hall, and the drawing room was at the end, windows overlooking the garden and conservatory, with the kitchen door next to it and a small door leading down to the cellar. Upstairs, there were four double bedrooms and a bathroom, with another small single bedroom halfway up the stairs – probably designed for living-in staff. Then on the top floor were two more bedrooms. I was given one of those. Moo (and Pa when he was at home) was given the room below me on the first floor. There was a second bed in my room, which would do nicely for Junie when she came on leave.

I suppose that I remember everything about this house so clearly because, by that time, I was 'looking' at everything with the eyes of a potential writer, jotting down notes all the time, making observations, thinking of ways to record small events that happened. The world was beginning to open up quite consciously for me, and it was almost as though I had a pair of antennae, like a snail, looking round at every tiny detail of just about everything. I could go back to The Avenue today and know exactly where everything in the neighbourhood was. It feels quite strange because I have lived in so many places in my life but this particular house is engraved into the deepest depths of my memory. Of course, there is a very good reason for this.

When Moo and I arrived at The Avenue in a taxi, Moo introduced me to Mrs McGavin, a charming person, who insisted that we all call her Nesta, and Nesta she became, even though Moo thought this very disrespectful of me to treat a Grown-Up with familiarity rather than respect. In her world, family friends were always known as Uncle and Aunt. Nesta showed us all over the house, enjoying Moo's pleasure at the spacious size of the bedroom that she and Pa would share, and I was delighted to be one floor above, in a smaller double room with a much better view over the sweep of the entrance drive, the Avenue, and the unexpectedly interesting rail track across the road down in its deep cutting. This window became my vantage point for keeping the Avenue under surveillance, exploring the skies for aircraft, which all had to be identified and written down in my AEROPLANE IDENTIFICATION book, as so many boys and girls did at that time; and for occasionally doing my best to drop 'water-bombs' on certain visitors. When Junie was on leave, she would share this room under the eaves of the house, which she did with a certain reserve, probably because I could not stop asking what life was like in the WRENS, what her job was and how many friends she had made – endlessly probing into what was now her private world, no doubt out of sheer envy. I settled quickly into our attractive bedroom filled, as it was, with light from two windows. Nesta had good taste in furnishings and the plain white brocade curtains were a perfect choice against walls that were papered with panels of ivy on trelliswork so that it all felt very rural and *al fresco*. The beds had white candlewick covers and there was a green flowered rug on the wood floor between the beds. Nesta had thoughtfully given us a pair of curve-backed Edwardian chairs with padded seats, covered with tapestry flowers, which I later realised she had woven herself. She loved doing tapestry work and seemed to have one on the go all the time. I liked Nesta the moment I met her. We clicked, and she began to plan how she could find companionable young friends of my age.

It did not take me long to unpack, stow my clothes away in the chest of drawers ('don't forget to leave a drawer empty for Junie,' Moo had directed) and arrange my Arthur Ransome treasures on a shelf between the two windows. I had left Rambler Cottage with three of the books he had given me, but only after a blazing row for them between Moo and Auntie Dee, who tried to insist that they should remain with her. Moo had been so incensed with the whole business of her daughter being accused of stealing and thrown out, that she did not mince her words, and once the books were in her hands, had physically hung onto them for dear life. She was of course a lot stronger than Auntie Dee where physical things were concerned. I was eternally grateful to her, because I had not been allowed to take the hot water bottle cover that Arthur Ransome had knitted for me. To my delight and gratitude, he then sent me his next two books as they were published, with a little message in them regretting my departure and hoping that all was well with us. I dare say Guiny gave him our address.

Those five books were my greatest treasures and I read them again and again, and every time I did, I came upon something that I had missed in the previous reading and this made me think all the harder about how I should write and what details should be explored. They became the text-books for learning about my own way of writing.

There were two other paying guests in the house; Mrs Brazil and her son Jack. Jack was exempted from being called-up because he had something the matter with his health, although I could never see what it was. He must have been in his thirties or more, and had joined the National Fire Service instead. Jack is a shadowy figure in my memory, which means that I never focused on him. He was, I think, quite tall, very polite and inclined to be bald – and that is the only impression of him that remains. Mrs Brazil is much more in focus because she was very elderly to my eyes, so probably not more than in her early sixties, but she was severely bent, always wore dark, old-fashioned clothes and crept around the place soundlessly, emanating an odd feeling of menace. She was not very sociable and seldom joined the McGavins and the Finlays in the drawing room in the evenings but appeared for meals, some of which she even took back to her bedroom. She had a married daughter and quite often spent a few days away in the country, staying with her. Jack did his duty hours with the Fire Service but joined us all when he was home in the evenings.

Colonel McGavin was not at all as we had expected, having met the elegantly slender Nesta. He was a stocky, not very tall man with a busy, fussy way of both walking and 'being.' He fidgeted in his chair when he talked, often cut across what others were saying, and seemed to have a very good opinion of himself. He was also clearly partly Anglo-Indian, which gave Moo quite a turn. Having been brought up in India, where segregation was *de rigueur*, her generation would, except in special circumstances, ignore anyone who was of mixed blood (unless they were of some eminence) and she was deeply embarrassed to discover that she was the house guest of a mixed-race person. Worse still, she was furious with Pa for not telling her (he had probably not even noticed). When it was casually let drop that in fact they were not married, our strait-laced Moo, brought up within rigid Victorian strictures by her own mother, was never the same with Nesta after that. It gradually transpired that there was a wife across the World in Ceylon, whom he had married at eighteen, but when he joined the British Army and came to Europe, he had never wanted to return there. These days there is, thank goodness, absolutely no importance attached to peoples' private arrangements but until about the mid-1950s there were a great many rules that had to be observed for every walk of Life. You might be thinking of Moo as being racist, but she and her generation had been brain-washed into following a very strict social code, and she was no different from most others of her peer group.

One day Nesta invited us over to Farnborough to meet her Father, Professor Fernau an Egyptologist, and her sister-in-law's family who lived with him. "She has two boys around your age, so I'm sure they'll be friendly in the holidays."

Nesta's father was as lovely as Nesta. Nesta's sister-in-law, Isobel Fernau, had a wasting disease. I do not know where her husband was, probably away in some War sector, but Isobel and her two sons, Christopher and Guy, lived in Farnborough, with their grandfather. When I first met the brothers in 1943, Christopher was at school at Repton and must have been about fifteen. Guy had just started public school at Canford, down in Dorset, so he must have been about thirteen; only a little older than me. They lived in a charming house with a garden and a long orchard, which reminded me of Guiny and her bees. I fell in love with old Professor Fernau right away. He seemed very aged and benign, requiring reverential treatment and complete attention. He was quite lame, and hunched his shoulders when he sat down, leaning forward to talk to his listener with such keen attention that you felt you were the only person in the world that he wanted to talk to. He had very large brown eyes that glowed at you from beneath bushy brows, and there was a single wild whisker on each eyebrow that was longer than the rest and curled upwards, giving him a slightly enquiring expression. Those brown eyes twinkled and danced and sometimes watered with mirth, and I am quite certain that this was the first time I felt real love for a stranger. I had never known my two grandfathers – but Grandad Fernau was the sort of grandfather that I would really have loved to have had. In no time he had discovered my passing interest in archaeology,[10] and started to show me his beautiful Egyptian artefacts, which were placed at strategic points all round the house. There were bowls and urns, miniature long-boats, and clay images of

---

[10] Pa had three archaeologist friends who had become some of my many 'uncles,' so I had begun to know quite a lot about English archaeology from both Sir Mortimer Wheeler, a colleague from Pa's Army days, and from an attractive young protégé of Uncle Mortie's called Glyn Daniel. Both became popular television hosts after the war. [DV]

serving women, boatmen and even animals. I always waited eagerly for Nesta to suggest we paid the Fernaus a visit because in a remarkably short time I took two of them to my heart with a passion that hit me like falling into a stone wall, and completely knocked me sideways.

I met the boys at the same time as Professor Fernau and felt nervous and self-conscious with them at first. Christopher was quite bossy, being the eldest of us all. Whatever Christopher and Guy thought of me, I decided that Guy was the one I had most in common with, and proceeded to fall in love from the heart for the first time in my short life. I was not aware that my feelings were the dreams that "Love" is made from. Guy was a gentle boy, kind and thoughtful, and who never teased me the way Christopher did. He was delighted with my fascination for his grandfather's Egyptology tales, and the questions I was always asking about the pharaohs and their elaborate lives. We started two collections, one of stamps and the other of shrapnel, which one could pick up off the road and in the gardens because of the continuing dog-fights that were, despite the end of the Battle of Britain, going on in the skies above us. We climbed trees, went for walks and Guy became the perfect companion. It was the first time in my whole life that I had had a real day-by-day friend who sought my company so regularly and obviously was delighted that I sought his too. I used to dream that we could see each other all day and night (except when I was in the bath or on the loo) and this stood me in good stead when term time loomed and away they went. Guy sent me, as well as various stamps swaps now and then, two post cards of the school from Canford, and I slipped them into the end covers of *Swallows and Amazons*, the safest place for such treasures.

I do not remember what Moo did to occupy herself during the day while we were at The Avenue. I had plenty to do because I attached myself to Nesta, who seemed to welcome this and I made myself useful. She was running a branch of the Red Cross in Beckenham Town Centre, and there seems to have been a great deal of paperwork. She had a large typewriter, a glorious instrument which she taught me to use (with two fingers), so that I could type out all the envelopes that had to be sent to members in a constant flow for her. It is where I learned to put the right amount of m's, t's and e's in the word Committee! The McGavins had a Morrison shelter in the study, which was a large indoor construction made with a solid steel table-top, welded mesh sides and steel legs and 'floor.' The purpose of this cumbersome 'table' was to be able sleep two in there during air raids, so that if the house fell on you, you would not be crushed. I'd have loved to have made a nest in there to go and do my 'thinking' in, but Nesta used every inch of the top as a desk, which was perfect for all her committee and Red Cross files and IN and OUT trays. There was another desk in the study but this was Colonel McGavin's domain, and was not to be touched under any circumstances, not even dusted! It's funny, now I come to think if it, but he was always 'Colonel McGavin', never Neville, which was his Christian name. Pa would call him things like 'old boy' or even 'sir' to make a point – but although Pa was 'Alan' to all their adult friends, the Colonel was The Colonel!

I had started term at a local day school, which wasn't to be for long, a fore-shadowing of what was to come. I still wonder why I cannot remember a thing about it, apart from the fact that we had brown coats and school hats. Pa and Junie came and went, Pa working then at

Bletchley Park and Junie away up in Weatherby, Yorkshire. Junie looked stunning in her smart WRNS uniform, as the family had known she would. It was clear that she was making plenty of friends and beginning to enjoy herself. At first I think the whole spectrum of mass indoctrination, learning to march in drilling exercises etc. were not to her liking as she had never enjoyed sporting activities of any kind, and marching up and down seemed a terrible waste of time to her, just as it had to Pa when he was her age. All the same, she made life-lasting friendships at this period in her life, especially with one girl called Mary Drax, whose real surname was Plunkett-Ernle-Earle Drax! June and Mary became firm friends, followed each other around with their WRNS postings and both, I *think,* ended up in the P5 section at Eastcote and then at Bletchley Park, though I may well be wrong there. Junie was born in 1926 and I think that Mary was fractionally older. Her father was an admiral in the Royal Navy with the astounding name of Sir Reginald Aylmer- Ranfurley- Plunkett-Ernle-Erle-Drax!

By the time Moo and I found ourselves in The Avenue, in the south of England but still part of the main London sprawl, our lives began to settle into a more manageable routine. I do not know how Moo resolved the financial black hole that her Batchworth Heath project had dropped us into, or how we were even able to pay for our accommodation because Pa's Army salary was very modest and there was no such thing in those days as the Marriage or Family Allowance, let alone any health cover; but someone or something must have rescued us. Moo had a small income of her own but I know that there were a lot of visits to lawyers in the City at that time. Various trusts had been set up for Pa when his grandfather Gedye, his father and then his mother and two aunts had died. They must all have been well aware that any money left to him would disappear into some marvellous but hugely costly invention that never saw the light of day, and so ensured that their legacies to him were tied up, to protect us, Pa's family, into unraidable trusts.

*

The War was just beginning to tilt in the direction of Britain and her allies and in May of that year the battle for North Africa was won and both Germany and Italy had to surrender their armies to the British and Allied armies. It was an absolute shot in the arm for us, and in July that year British and American forces landed in Sicily and fought their way up into the toe of Italy. At another level entirely, 1943 was also the year that penicillin, having been invented in 1928 by British scientist Alexander Fleming but marketed in the USA, was first imported back into the UK, firstly to cure Winston Churchill of pneumonia, and then to be used widely in military hospitals where it saved, and continues to save, countless thousands of lives. Winning the Battle of Britain in 1940 gave the RAF the adrenaline it needed to bring up its other fighter and bomber squadrons. And success in the air continued for our young fighter aces. In January 1943 the RAF made their first daylight bombing raid on Berlin, and later in the same year began a serious winter campaign against Germany's great Capitol Berlin. The British army and her Allies stormed through southern Italy and on the 8th September, Italy announced its surrender, having backed the wrong horse, and realizing that if they did not retire from this destructive combat, their armies as well as their priceless historical treasures would be destroyed in the wave of the ferocious continuing battles that were plundering through their beautiful country. The Royal Navy and her Canadian, Australian, Indian and American counterparts proceeded to patrol the oceans, aided by new radar systems, with something secret going on at Bletchley Park, so that finally German Admiral Donitz was forced to pull his U-boats out of the North Atlantic altogether. The War was on the turn.

The entire British population went to the cinema at least once a week in those days. The cinema and the wireless, as radio was called then, were what most families did for leisure because, food and drink becoming ever scarcer, parties were mostly to be found in the various Army, Navy and RAF messes, or in the municipal dance halls in every town, large or small. If you did not dance, or drink, or could not leave your home, then music and humour on the BBC was almost all you could find for your leisure listening time. There were several comedy BBC programmes, which we all looked forward to each week, mostly because they not only had a catchy signature tune but were peppered with a series of oft-repeated phrases that we soon were on the look-out for, and which we all exchanged together in daily conversation. A comedian called Tommy Handley had one of the most popular weekly comedies called "It's That Man Again…", which was soon shortened to ITMA. I can still sing the signature tune – and am humming it now. Tommy was a great character and ensured that there were plenty of hilarious personalities to be introduced in the course of the programme. I won't bore you with them here but all of these wartime cartoon radio characters wormed their way into our lives, and they continue to live on, in the heads of those of us who are still alive today. A 21st century reader may well know the names of programmes such as 'The Goon Show' and 'Round The Horn' etc. Those programmes were the *remnants* of the of those older comedies originally created to lift the depressed spirits of the population when the 2nd world war was at its lowest. I expect, if you search 'Gert & Daisy' you will discover that they were two hilarious Cockney ladies (sisters of actor Jack Warner) called Elsie and Doris Waters who kept British housewives laughing through their programme 'The Kitchen Front'. They even published a cookery book. Then there was Arthur Askey and Richard Murdoch's 'Band Waggon' – and so on. They not only kept our spirits up, but gave us certain 'catchphrases' to exchange with each other knowingly – which everyone, from dustman to Duke, soon did liberally. King George V1 is recorded as having said of ITMA, "We always listen." There was ITMA's daily help, Mrs Mopp, who would come into the studio and say "Can I do you now, sir?" and of course any amount of suggestive connotations could be attached to this, and they were! It was not long before the cleaning ladies in every household fortunate enough to have one was called a 'Mrs Mopp'. Such was the power of the wireless in wartime.

*

Nesta encouraged me to write down my thoughts, dreams, poetry – everything – so much so that I finally settled into the love of the written word, and began to find the ability to express myself. She took me over to Farnborough at least twice a week and I spent an hour or more with Grandad Fernau, listening to the marvelous way he had of painting word pictures of the days of the Pharoahs, and backing this up with taking me through his collections of precious artefacts. During the school holidays Guy was usually in attendance too, and it was through looking over Guy's stamp collection that I became interested and decided to start one of my own, very much encouraged by Nesta who pointed out that it would be a great help where History and Geography was concerned. Chris, thank goodness, was more likely to be off doing something else. It is interesting just how positive I felt about both those brothers. You could say that I didn't exactly dislike Chris, because I had no real reason for doing so, as he could be quite friendly at times. But at other times he would tease and poke me, which I found really irritating and so became a bit uncomfortable in his presence. Guy was natural, friendly and treated me as though I was another boy – except that he smiled at me a lot, which I loved, and discovered my pulse revving up a gear when he did this. I think I am happy to have been born when I was because the sweet memories of those innocent courting days are some of the most precious and tender memories I have now.

1944 was a pivotal year of change for me and for Britain. We were by then so very short of all commodities, of food and clothing, as well as basic materials like fuel, steel and manpower. On the 18th January the very first conscripts of what became known as The Bevin Boys started their training to be sent down the mines if they were not, for one reason or another, able to be called up for National Service in the armed forces.[11]   In the

---

[11] They were so named after Ernest Bevin, the Socialist Minister of Labour in the wartime coalition government, who created this division to

meantime, Britain and her Allies began preparing for the greatest sea-born Invasion of one Nation by another since history was recorded. The adults must have been aware that 'something was going on' for some time before Operation Overlord took place, because there was gradually an increase in military movements in the South of England, with large convoys of vehicles shifting from place to place as they manoeuvred into position for the big assault.

I became aware of this strange behaviour when, one day, a huge convoy of Army vehicles appeared in The Avenue and lined the entire road on the open railway side. They crept in overnight, coming into our midst quietly, with no revving motors, no diesel fumes, remaining with us for a week, and then disappearing in the same way, when darkness cloaked their movements. There were hundreds of soldiers with the lorries, armoured cars and tanks all forms of mobile militaria. The men were pensive, even subdued, and although the house owners chatted to them as they tended their vehicles or just sat and appeared to be waiting, they seemed to have their minds on other things and few of them accepted cups of tea or any refreshments. Their officers were constantly moving up and down between the vehicles, talking quietly to the men in groups, and without seeming to have anything to do, they were very occupied all the same. Guy and I proudly showed our growing collection of shrapnel to the men in the lorry outside the house and I was tremendously excited when,

---

assist and increase man-power in the various mines. The following month in February the very first announcement was made about the Government's plans to create a National Health Service in the future, created by a rival labour minister Aneurin Bevan, with whom he is often confused. [DV]

casting around the gutters in Copers Cope Road nearby, I found the tail fin of an oil bomb – which became our most prized possession. One of the soldiers did a drawing of the whole oil bomb and explained to us what it was made of, and its particular purpose, long since forgotten now! I was so interested in this great Convoy; a silent serpent of khaki magnificence with its covered guns, oil-smelly tanks, busy little armoured cars nipping around between one convoy and the next, that Moo finally forbade me to go out and talk to the soldiers any more. "What will they think of you?" She said. "You are behaving like the women who follow the troops around. I'm sure that red-haired one is eyeing you up and down, and I won't have it."

I had not noticed anyone giving me special attention, red-haired or any other colour but, looking back now; I was thirteen years old, my body must have been steadily maturing, and it had to be agreed that recently Moo had been discussing the fact that I would soon have to wear a bra. I was still blissfully unaware of the effect of this growth – not even with the lovely Guy. If any of the soldiers had been chatting me up, the 13-year-old Dione was not aware of it. However, the ban on talking to the soldiers was not to last for long because when I woke one morning, very shortly after that conversation, the whole enormous convoy had gone. I had not heard the sound of their engines starting up during the night, though Moo said that she had, and in a strange way, the empty road made us all feel that we had lost something unique and precious. When Moo and I heard on the wireless that all those endless military vehicles, waiting patiently for their orders to move in the road outside our door, had been preparing for The Invasion of France, we and everyone else in The Avenue were filled with pride and of course wished that we had been allowed to pay them more attention. We stayed close to every news bulletin because every hour that passed, there were fresh reports about the promising progress of our armies. I think my schoolwork must have been forgotten because I know I stayed close to Moo and the wireless for those early days after D-Day. Messages from both Pa and Junie both by now at Bletchley Park, indicated that they were too busy for leave and we were too excited by everything going on so few miles away across the channel to even miss them. The weather had been really dismal with summer storms and grey skies, and, now I come to think of it, I must have been brewing a cold because Moo had to go to the chemist on the second day after D-Day to get something called Thermogene for my chest.

Days later, I heard noises outside, with neighbours calling to each other, pointing at the sky. Nesta and I went out into the drive and stood watching a tiny speck moving across the horizon with two other specks accompanying it. No - that wasn't right. Even as I focussed on the distant aircraft, one of them shot ahead, turned in a tight arc and flew directly at the central plane. Tiny puffs of grey smoke ringed it in a cotton-wool halo and even as the rear fighter banked and turned to do the same manoeuvre, the distant sound of its gunfire reached us. The central aircraft flew onwards without faltering. It was clearer now and I could hear the sound of its engines, a deep woolly drone.

Shouts of encouragement and hoots of delight went up from the watching neighbours as something must have hit. As the three aircraft got closer, we could see a distinct but thin, bright feather of flame pouring from the oddly uplifted tail. The two fighters buzzed furiously round the enemy plane, swooping, jiggling their wings, the tracer from their guns cleaving the quiet morning air like pebbles rattling in a tin can. The enemy plane ignored its feverish attackers completely and flew onward. I watched the dog-fight as it streamed away towards London - and then without warning the bubbly drone of its deep engines suddenly ceased. I couldn't help jumping up and down in excitement as the two spitfires circled their prey. In silence the enemy aircraft sailed on - and then, just as suddenly its nose went down and it plummetted out of the sky in a vertical drop, showing its stubby wings. We were beginning to cheer and wave at the triumphant Spitfires when there was an almighty explosion, which stopped us all in our tracks. Moo came running from the kitchen.

The All Clear sounded then and we returned to our morning tasks without further incident but I couldn't get the little plane out of my mind for the remainder of that day. The deep rough note of its engines had sounded odd and quite different to any of the other aircraft, and it wasn't on my aeroplane identification book. Why had the enemy plane caused such a violent blast? It was quite a small aircraft, and had crashed quite a long way away from us. We watched the two Spits circling….. circling over the area, and then they leapt back into the sky and were gone, leaving us quite mystified. All became clear when we heard the lunchtime news, because the first of these flying bombs had landed early that morning before daylight, exploding on impact and destroying a railway bridge and killing six people. Five more had been reported and others were being attacked throughout the day. It was the first day of the World's first cruise missile war, a period which lasted until March 1945 and which brought havoc and dread into our lives, as no other weapon ever did on British soil. On the 18th June, a Flying Bomb, which were variously known as V1s, Buzz Bombs and Doodle Bugs, landed on the Guards Chapel in Wellington Barracks, during a service. The explosion destroyed the whole building and killed 121 people, injuring 141 others. But Moo and I were not aware of what was happening by then because Beckenham's first Doodle Bug had already left its mark. It was decided that if this was to be a daily business we had better furnish the cellar with as many comforts as possible, including candles and torches. I took down a couple of chairs as we only had an old sofa there and Moo threw me three packets of candles and some matches from the top of the cellar steps.

It was such a lovely surprise when Junie turned up with a quick 24-hour Pass, to thank us for the birthday gifts we had sent her. She had been stationed up in Weatherby in Yorkshire but had been transferred to Eastcote in Middlesex the month before. She was full of the news that they had had a share in getting the Invasion Force over to France, so her whole group had celebrated not only her 19th birthday but also D-Day – but now many of them were being moved to Bletchley Park, where Pa had been for some time and which seemed less likely to be within striking distance of these frightening new flying bombs. She had not had any experience of them and so was both interested and fearful when the next one came bumbling over us, gurgling and coughing its deep, resonant engine sound. I had begun to listen out for them because it was clear that we must be on their flight path, or pretty close to it because they would be seen passing to our left in the distance, or to our right – and now and then one would actually pass right over us. We were beginning to get a little anxious because it was becoming clear that they were likely to do one of two things. When the engine stopped – and there was that awful heavy silence in our ears, the flying bomb would either float gently down and sometimes travel for quite a distance before impact – or else it would tip over and drop like a stone upon whatever was beneath it when its motor died. Our luck had so far held because one of them had been right overhead, and for about a minute we seemed to be frozen to the spot, Moo and Nesta and me: out in the middle of the drive and frighteningly aware that there was nowhere for us to run to. Thankfully, the awful thing floated on, not even seeming to lose height, until Nesta said breathlessly.

"Inside – quick. Cellar." And the three of us just ran. Mrs Brazil never came outside with us and we fled past her in the hall, making for the cellar stairs beside the kitchen door. The explosion came before Nesta had time to open it, and everything shook and in the kitchen something fell into the sink with a crash.

"Phew." Nesta said as the explosion faded. She and Moo stared at each other with relief. "That was close. I really don't think we should watch them anymore, do you? They are likely to fall on us before we can get down into the cellar."

Mrs Brazil joined us, looking shaken.

"I think I shall go and stay with my daughter in Anglesey." She said. "It isn't safe here anymore." We were all aware that this was now the case, even me – who had tended to think of it all as another adventure until a moment before. I cannot remember any more close shaves that day and indeed, apart from a vague memory of the garden at that time of the year — colour and warmth and delicious scents in the air — I dare say I was happy to nurse my chesty cold out in the dappled sunlight of the orchard, dreaming of the charm of Guy. Maybe I was also plotting impossible short stories from the rope hammock that Colonel McGavin had put up between two ancient apple trees.

CHAPTER SEVEN

Down and Out

The morning of June 15th was much the same as any other summer morning. I woke when Moo called up the stairs to me at 7.30am and spent the usual few minutes clearing my airways, which always seemed to be blocked for days after a cold. Blocked airways are quite frightening if you are asthmatic because they can suddenly become acutely blocked if you try to clear them in a hurry and then you're headed for real trouble. These days we have Clenil Modulate and Salbutamol inhalers to ease the problem, but there was nothing of that sort in my childhood and the death rate through Asthma was high.

I washed and dressed, pulled back my bedding to let it air, and went down to the kitchen to help with getting breakfast onto the dining table. There would only be three of us this morning as Colonel McGavin was away, Mrs Brazil had left to go to her daughter in Anglesey the day before, her son Jack was still on night duty with the Fire Service and Pa and Junie were now up in Bletchley Park together for the first time. I took the tray containing all our rations into the dining room. Everyone had their own labeled pots and dishes for butter, jam, cheese and anything else that needed our ration cards, and so there were two long trays in the cool larder in which everything was kept.

Although we were only three, we still ate in the dining room. Today I dare say we'd have laid breakfast out in the kitchen, but that was never even considered back in the 1940s. I do not recall what we ate that morning but I would imagine it was the same as we usually had. Some fruit from the garden, when there was any, a boiled or poached egg on toast, and toast with plum jam, made from last year's plum crop, all washed down with either tea or a quite disgusting coffee made from what tasted like tree bark. Horrible!

Nesta and I got on really well, even if Moo had become rather distant and 'polite' with our hostess by then and so breakfast, when there were just the three of us, would be accompanied by comfortable chat in which I was central, despite Moo's edict that "children should be seen and not heard" – I was by this time quite tall, even beginning to be shapely, and no longer considered myself a child. I have come to realise much later in life that Moo had been a marvelous mother of her daughters when they were small but, having no younger siblings of her own, only much older ones – and all males too - she had little idea of how to guide older girls who were on the threshold of adulthood. Fortunately for Junie, her beauty and intelligence seemed to slightly inhibit Moo and she rarely tried to tell her what to do because that seemed to be Pa's roll – guiding Junie. Moo was content to cherish her first-born with devotion and constant amazement that she had actually created this perfect young woman; and all through their lives she was never heard to question anything that Junie did, whether it was good or bad. Dookie, on the other hand, was another subject entirely. Because I had been so indulged by the nuns from the age of three, I had become a real rebel if I could not get my own way, and there was a constant battle between Moo, doing her best with this difficult child, and me, who wanted so much to learn and spread my wings – and Moo was not capable of answering most of the many questions I was always asking her. "Why….." I would ask and back came Moo's standard answer – "Because, that's why." And I was left frustrated and determined never to let that word pass my lips with my own children. The result in my own youth was that Moo was always quite short with me, and I was usually quite grumpy with her. Nesta was the perfect foil for this situation because she had obviously found something to be fond of in me and, through patient discussion and advice, was beginning to discover a different Dione entirely. She was fond of Moo too, despite her thinly veiled disapproval of the situation with Colonel McGavin. Nesta generously took Moo's polite charm at face value even though she would not have realised just how difficult being married to Pa was, let alone trying to cope with bringing up her daughters on a shoestring.

On this particular morning we seemed to have lingered over breakfast for some time and both Nesta and Moo were still in their dressing gowns; Moo had a padded blue silk one with pink dogs on it, which Pa had given her years before, and Nesta always wore her green Paisley silk peignoir. Having cleared the table when we were done and helped Nesta to dry up the breakfast things, I had not yet gone upstairs to make my bed when the air raid warning sounded. At that time the alert sounded whenever a Flying Bomb was spotted, and the All Clear went once it was past our area, but I'm told that this did not last long because soon there were too many flying bombs coming over, sometimes at a rate of one every few minutes – but that was long after this particular day.

Nesta had gone into the study, Moo was in the kitchen and I was on the first step of the stairs when the Alert sounded.

"Dook, don't go up. Go to the cellar and I'll be right behind you." Moo must have been putting something away. I opened the cellar door, switched on the light and clattered down into the cool dry depths that went under most of the house. I sat myself down in the ancient sofa. The chairs were close together with a table on which stood a jerry can filled with water; and a tray beside it had an assortment of cups and mugs, a pile of plates and several knives. As I reached out to pour some water into a mug, I saw Moo's pink-slippered feet coming down to join me, the pink and blue of her dressing gown bright from the light behind her – and in that instant there was a huge, enormously metallic, catastrophic WHOOOOOSH, and pressure thundering against my eardrums like the punch of giant boxing gloves.

My mind registered a brief image of Moo tumbling down the cellar steps with all the tennis racquets and coils of spare electric cable that hung on the walls beside the door smashing into her, winding around her, cutting across the shocked white orb of her face; I was lifted by a giant hand in the thunderous void and flung hard against the far wall among the Colonel's crates of wine. My head seemed to explode like a water melon – and then there was nothing................

Sensation..... encased in something shifting, rock-hard and stabbing, which gauged and crushed and penetrated..........nothing, but then something; nostrils blocked with what felt like wool, my chest struggling to find something to breathe in; choking..... nothing..... pain, always pain - but there was no breath to cry out, only thick acrid dust that caked my nose and mouth dust everywhere ..... then sightless, billowing nothing......

I have no idea how long that 'nothing' lasted, seconds or hours, but at some point I registered that everything was in total darkness until I realised that my eyelids must still be shut because there were misty floating patterns with flashing star points all round me. I did my best to focus on them and then there was nothing again...... I must have returned to consciousness and realised that there was something very heavy and hot cutting into my back and my shoulder – my face hurt, and the air was almost solid with evil-smelling brick dust. I tried to open my eyes but it felt as though fingers were pressing them closed. I tried to move my mouth to keep the almost solid dust out of my lungs, and to lift my arms. I found it was possible to move the right one fractionally, and was able to pull the right side of my cardigan across my nose and mouth so that I could breathe through it. Terror only came gradually, as pain rolled in over my body as though I was being flattened by a steam roller; maybe I was… I wept inside my head but there was no air to draw into my lungs for expressing sound, and the 'nothing' scooped me up again…. I was dying and it didn't matter because there was no future, no life there anymore… and then there was nothing again. Time had not been created for this sort of experience and so did not exist.

There came a period when the dust seemed to settle and I was able to take a tiny, fractional shallow breath now and then without choking. It allowed me to become aware of SOUND - the invisible infinity of density and of shifting things. I could not turn my head in one direction but there seems to have been a bit of space on the right side, where my arm was not pinioned against something, as the rest of me was. It took an eternity to realise that I had actually been able to open one eye without anything disastrous happening to the eyeball – but the left eyelid was stuck closed so I forgot about that. All concentration was honed on checking whether I was alive or dead. Ian, never far from me since birth, pointed out in my head that if I was dead there would be no need for the great waves of pain that ebbed and flowed through me, if I even tightened a muscle, like storm waves dashing against the rocks. I tried to shift my left shoulder and hot knives plunged into me, tipping the whole red awfulness back into nothing…..

The body's instinct for survival seems to be an extraordinary one. Consciousness and belief in Ian's abiding support made my brain review the option in a cool and calculating way which had little to do with being a child or an adult. I was NOW and it seemed important to resist losing the present. I was aware that I existed but blind to whatever was out there beyond my eyelids, if only I could open them.

*

MOO! I must have had an intake of breath with the shock of remembering Moo flooding into my head, because even through the cardigan my mouth and chest filled with acrid-tasting dust-laden air and the coughing began again. I coughed and coughed, and gasped – and tried to control the spasm, and held onto the cardigan against my mouth and did my best to take tiny, tiny intakes of breath; and I stayed alive and began to realise that there was less dust in what was going into my lungs, and in that same moment knew – really knew that Moo must be near me. I had no breath just then to call out, only to cough and struggle to keep those minute shallow intakes through my cardigan going, so that I did not float away again – and then I heard something.

"Dookie…..Dookie……"

She was alive! My heart reared in my chest; the whole bubble of my existence filled with tears and I could feel them inching down my right cheek and the left eye wept into the hard something that was against that side of my face. I made myself breathe at the top of the cough so that whatever it was that was making me cough was not agitated. You can become remarkably technical in these moments when your life is on a thread and you are absolutely aware of it in a cold detached way. I concentrated, with Ian's voice encouraging me every step of the way on getting some sort of oxygen into my lungs, and every now and then I heard her voice.

"Dookie...... Dookie........"

I do not know how long it was before that stealthy shifting and sliding of hugely menacing invisible things gradually ceased. At one point something hit me sharply on my free shoulder and then slid past, leaving pain in a new area of me but it did not have any impact because I was existing in one solid red tidal wave of pain. The only all-consuming necessity was to breathe.

Time was just blackness. Thick, shifting, creaking blackness overlain with the solid stench of mould of old house foundations with which my cardigan-filtered air was impregnated.

"Dookie, please talk, please, please.............." There was a sob in that disembodied voice which was heart-breaking; fear and grief as well as the gasps of her own pain. She thought I was dead – but 'I'm here Mookie, I'm here and I'm alive and so are you....' nothing again.... And then I became aware that I was trying to call out but all that came through the cardigan over my mouth was a pathetic croak that was not even a word, let alone a pennant of hope for her. The throbbing shoulder and pain in my chest and arm seemed to be a little less furious, so I tried again, projecting words on the outgoing mini-breath to try and send it out of my body this time.

"Mookie...." and then "OK..."

From somewhere close by in the tumbled hiatus of unseen black destruction and chaos I heard another little sob, and she wept quietly until I heard, "Oh thank God. Thank God…" and it felt as though I had been lifted up out of that hideous grave and brought back to my Mother, where the person outside of the present me, and who had been Dione, knew I was not dead. I had to let her know I was all right but….

"Can't breathe….." I croaked, spitting out a mouth full of debris. "breathing through my cardigan………"

"Good…good" came back after a pause, something far away shifted and the earth miles below us trembled and we must both have frozen in case this was that moment, after all.

"Your chest, Dookie. Does your chest hurt?" My heart felt fine. It was hammering like a train with the shock of the explosion and I could hear the blood singing in my ears - but there was no sign of that familiar dragging pain, no tell-tale uneven note in the rhythm of its beat. There was plenty of pain in my left shoulder, I suddenly realised, and hissed as I tried to lift my arm.

"Chest fine - left arm and shoulder very sore." I said grimly.

"Say a prayer…" Moo's voice seemed far away now - floating. "Say a prayer…a prayer….a prayer….and her voice echoed, hollow and receding…..nothing again….. later there was more movement a long way off but the silence was less filled with hissing debris, and then there was only Moo's voice and mine, and Ian became mute. We must have been quite close to each other but I could not reach my right arm out further than being able to waggle my hand and put it against my chest and then my cheek. I felt the wetness of my tears, my nose was flattened and something hurt in my head, something over my eye but they still did not matter; only the shallow precious breaths of ancient clotted air. Hang onto NOW, seemed to be what I must do.

Air and 'now' was all that mattered.

We croaked at each other like toads in a pond and there was still no such thing as time, only our pain and those fluid periods of 'nothing' in between.

"Call for help…..." Moo said at one point. And she called, and now and then when I had blown away whatever was piled up around my cardigan, I tried to call too. I found I could open both eyes and the crowded black void seemed very slightly less total until dust quickly closed them again.

"Can you see anything," I asked because I was sure I could see someone moving in the monstrous 'nothing' all round me.

"No – been calling for ages….. throat's raw. Thought I heard a voice - but … nothing since then."

She seemed to have more air than I had, because the strain in her voice was not from being clogged up with brick and cement dust, as I was. I sensed that she was more hurt than she was telling me. She began to call again and I did my best to join in, using my frog's croak – but at least it was a sound.

In one of the moments when we paused to rest our tortured lungs, I heard a new sound. Drip…drip…drip…

".... water." I said. "We'll be drowned."

It was suddenly something to be terrified of and I tried to struggle against what was imprisoning me, touching the sides, no movement, no escape, pressing in, great flames of pain lapped through me, eating my flesh so that I gasped, head now spinning, taking in too much dust-laden air, and my throat went into spasm and closed down ...

*

Up in The Avenue, the fire brigade, half a dozen Air Raid Wardens, a St. John's Ambulance team and a group of neighbours were moving around, hauling wreckage aside as they looked for survivors. They worked on what had been the front and side of the house for some time before someone called across and said they thought they had heard a voice calling. Silence was made absolute and then they heard Moo calling, faint and deep down – and the chief warden got his megaphone and shouted down into the wreckage.

Head throbbing, the space around pulsing now far away, then close and far again. Focus! I could hear voices – was Moo talking to someone?

"Keep calling," a distant voice said, "that is the only way we are going to be able to get to you." We were alive and others knew we were. Hope surging then it struck me.

NESTA.

My heart seemed to lurch and stop altogether – Nesta had been in the study just before the bang. She was up there somewhere, beyond the slammed cellar door; hurt by the blast - maybe lying in the hall with half the house on her and no one to help.

"Nesta!" I called frantically. "Nesta, we're here. Are you all right?" but I didn't get the words out before that other darkness found me again.

Choking coughing, the spinning stopped.

"Moo!" I had found my voice again.

"Mookie – wake up" nothing but the hiss of settling dust or was it just my ears hissing?

"Keep talking love…" that distant voice was back

"Oh do hurry, do hurry. Please God, save us, let them get here SOON."

"We're running a tunnel in from the road, Love. You say you're in the cellar. Can you make a guess how far from the road?"

Panic "I don't know – I can't see…"

I thought hard. "About twenty yards. My mother is close to the cellar door on the steps. I am next to the Morrison Shelter…"

Banging of metal tools, hammering, digging, scraping. Debris shifted ominously at the far end of the cellar and a shower of brick and plaster crashed down, throwing up another billow of choking dust. I coughed into my arm, eyes streaming but Moo was also hawking and inhaling lung-fulls of dust.

"Mookie!"

"All this dust!"

"Don't worry. They're coming to get us out right now."

"You are a brave little monster, after all." She said softly.

"You are too."

I felt proud of us both because we had not panicked once, not really. "I love you very much Moo."

"I know you do."

"Hurry up, Please - PLEASE." I yelled through the darkness. "My mother is'nt well. She needs a doctor."

"Doing our very best, Love." Was the voice a fraction closer?

Another cascading rumble this time from behind me, jabbing my shoulder, fighting the spinning – focus on Moo, the tremor subsided. Something had changed. There is something very protective about total darkness when you are confined to the area of your own consciousness and beyond that is the alien unknown. A sudden chink of white light appeared to one side of me which Moo could see too and our world changed in that instant.

Down and Out

20 - Aftermath of a V-1 bombing, London 1944 "a distant cheer" (HMSO public domain photograph)

"I can see light," she called to the diggers and there was a distant cheer, far away in the pure clean air above us. We could see dark shadows around ourselves for the first time aware suddenly of our situation. The faint light picked up Moo's ashen face just an arm's length away, a cut on her forehead oozing black blood over her temple. Her eyes were enormous, the orbs all pupil, sunk back into their skull sockets, her lashes and eyebrows clotted with white dust. She looked like a night creature shocked by sudden light. She stared at me fearfully, her cheeks streaked with rusty, dust-laden tears. She was completely white, like a spectre in a crypt, a shocking sight until I realised that she was covered with plaster dust - that we must both be. she said in a wobbly voice.

"I think I've hurt my leg. I can't seem to move it."

It was pinned against the floor by an enormous beam which had fractured in the middle. It was not until I saw that beam and the jagged teeth of its split that the weight of three floors came home to me pressing down. Fear froze my movements for a second until I forced myself to concentrate on Moo. Her leg was caught fair and square at the shin, above the ankle. We stared at it together and she stopped sniffing.

My shoulder began to throb and I could feel it swelling in the sleeve of my cardigan but the rest of me was unscathed apart from a long gash down the side of my leg. I looked at the blood oozing like tar through the tear in my stocking.

"Oh dear, I've ruined my new stockings and we haven't any coupons left." Moo sniffed beside me she was actually smiling.

"If we ever get out of here, you won't have to worry about coupons. They'll give us extra points and everything, I expect." I think we both laughed then.

It seemed important then to go on talking. We both sensed it and pursued the subject, trying to make little jokes as both of us knew that Nesta would have done but avoiding talking about her for fear of extinguishing any hope. We turned our eyes away from the sagging roof and the mountain of rubble at the end of the cellar where the light was coming from. It was then that I became aware that what was jabbing into my shoulder was the corner of the Morrison shelter. Somehow, it had punched through the floor of the study into the cellar sloping up towards the light which filtered through it. The back of my hand felt a very faint draught of air. Far away above our heads something was beginning to crumble. Slowly, beyond the protective floor, the house was settling in death. At the far end of the cellar a stream of rubble suddenly shifted and Moo's eyes flew open.

*

Then all quiet again, except the continuous drip of water. So cold – why so cold? Far far away, in that other place above our heads the crumbling sounds but I was drifting again.

I prayed and prayed to that comfortable Jesus of my childhood, the Jesus who had lived in the garden of my soul. "How overgrown it must be now", I thought. "If only you will get us out of here, I'll make it so tidy and sparkling that you'll never recognise it." I vowed. There was suddenly a great deal to live for, much more than I had noticed before - and all Nesta's patience and guidance would never again be wasted. I promised. And when I looked up I could no longer see Moo but we were just talking?

Slowly her shape emerged as the dust settled, her eyes still closed. She had dozed off - or maybe she was unconscious? I had never seen an unconscious person before.

"Moo!"

No response. Suppose she was dead? The blue frill of her nightie was still moving regularly - or she could be dying?

Sound of distant voices shouting above. Moo's eyes were still closed.

The house shifted and settled inwards again, sending down another heavy brickfall beside the coal-shute, restoring the darkness again and I shivered and waited for it to stop. The light from the Morrison shelter had got dimmer – no, it was flickering.

"Hello, down there...are you still OK?"

The voice was definitely closer and it seemed to be coming, not from beyond the cellar door now, but from the Morrison Shelter itself.

"Oh, please hurry." I called, suddenly giving way to the enormity of our situation. "Everything is coming in on us. Water, bricks - everything."

It was so very cold now and fear screamed through me with such force that I hid my eyes from the rubble wall. I could make out that Moo was shivering violently, as though someone was shaking her and the smallness, the vulnerability of her, steadied me. She was trapped by the leg and my left shoulder couldn't move. I reached out to her with my right hand, as yet again as a fresh fall of rubble cascaded across the floor, restoring the darkness. I listened out for Moo's faint breath and the thud of my own heart beats.

"Come on." Ian said. "Don't make such heavy weather of your situation. Pick out some beautiful words and think about them." I scoured the corridors of memory, clenching my teeth to stop them from chattering. The trembling in Moo's body went through us both and the cold moist ground was like lying on ice.

"On the mountains of the Prairie,

On the great Red Pipe-stone Quarry,

156

Down and Out

> Gitche Manito, the mighty,
>
> He the Master of Life, descending
>
> On the red crags of the quarry
>
> Stood erect, and called the nations,
>
> Called the tribes of men together..."

Funny how even the magic of those words was diminished by our danger. My shoulder, throbbing up and down the left side from neck to fingertips, was growing stiff so that even my jaw ached. Moo stirred in the darkness.

"Are we still here? Mother of God, what a nightmare. Will we ever get out?"

She sounded like a tremulous child and I tried to control the strangled voice which answered her, fighting to master my own panic of the terrible, pressing darkness.

"They are really near now, I promise. Listen hard and you'll hear their voices." I lied. There was a sudden monumental shifting in the thunderous darkness which seemed to come from the very foundations of the house, something struck the side of my head and I went spinning away from that place, turning, sliding swallowed by nothingness...

I was cold, stiff as a board - too stiff even to shiver. I had been cast in bronze. I was a statue - worse, I was dead. No, I could hear the blood singing steadily through me, through the high-pitched whistle in my ears, through the tight band round my chest. Something jerked me forward and I felt hands on my wrists. Another movement forward and a vicious blow across my mouth. Blood welled up along my gums, filled my throat. I swallowed and felt the jagged edge of broken tooth against my tongue. Another pull forward and then a sliding backwards into that vast floating void.

Air on my face.

Pain in my chest. I was coughing, retching, spinning and someone was pummelling my back. I was bent over on my side coughing - coughing against a distant buzz of voices.

"That's it, there's my girl - well done, cough it all up, nasty dust, that's what it is. Like another sip of water? That's the ticket. Now, just let me put this blanket round you and we'll have you into the ambulance in a jiffy."

I opened my eyes and closed them against harsh white light. Hands wrapping me tenderly in blankets, lifting me. I screamed as agony shot from my shoulder to my chest.

"Mind my shoulder...Where's Moo? Moo - I must see my mother..."

"Just stay quiet for half a mo' while I get this dressing on you, dear. You've busted your shoulder, by the look of things. Never mind, we'll soon have you feeling more comfy. You might have been far worse off."

The prick of a needle, a blessed floating drowsiness; faint awareness without concern, pain without awareness, movement without direction.

Next time I opened my eyes, the weary, kindly face of a VAD[12] was inches from my own. She crinkled her eyes at me.

"Good girl, just lie quietly and we'll have you in the hospital in a few minutes."

"Moo." I said and my voice was hoarse with brick dust. "Have they got my mother out? Is she all right?"

She smiled, patting my clutching hand on the woolly sleeve of her jacket. "They were just bringing her out as we left." She said. "They had to saw through ever such a big beam to free her but she's all right. Miraculous really, getting both of you out like that. You'll be able to see her as soon as we've tidied you up and got that shoulder dressed."

I floated away then, safe in the knowledge that Moo was out - that she was still in this world with me. She hadn't been taken away...[13]

---

[12] Voluntary Aid Detachment, WWII first aid volunteers [GL]

[13]Eventually, with the help of a hoist, they took a chunk of chimney out and found a corner of the shelter. At the same time they found Nesta but we were not told about that. It was halfway through the afternoon before they were able to talk to Moo, and another hour before they were able to get first me out, using the still unbuckled Morrison shelter as a sort of tunnel. They then had to take a steel joist off part of Moo's chest before they could bring her up through the Morrison shelter. It was probably about six in the evening before the two of us were back in the blessedly pure air, examined, patched up in the ambulance, rushed off to Beckenham hospital and, in due course, wired to oxygen, broken bones set in plaster, wounds dressed and settled in hospital beds where we slept and began to heal.

I am told that the Morrison shelter probably saved our lives because, in view of the angle it had fallen, right through the study floor with half the house on top of it, they were able to slide through it to Moo and me. It was a

The darkness of my sleep was a different colour to the smothering darkness in the cellar, to the terrible claustrophobia of being hauled out of the rubble. That stifling sensation, body compressed on all sides, nose, mouth - everything blocked by choking dust, no air, no room for my lungs to breathe. That was locked into memory, sealed by terror. Now the darkness was pure

21 - A Morrison Shelter (HMSO public domain photograph)

frightening thought though, that if the shelter had come plunging through the floorboards a couple of feet further to the left, it would have crushed us both.

They reached me first, and I think I sort of remember flashing lights, and voices and someone touching me, and then someone pulling me – by the arm that was so painful, and I knew I was screaming in my head but maybe that was just a dream. The pain must have knocked me out again because there is no memory of being brought up to the surface, through the Morrison shelter and out into the road, where the Ambulance men took charge. The rescue team went back down into the gap I had left and there was Moo, so close to me and yet we had felt so far away from each other. They brought her up the same way, and how very fortunate we were to find ourselves later that day, lying in clean hospital beds beside each other, strapped up and dosed with Oxygen and Morphine so that we relaxed and slept away the terrible hours that had gone before. [DV]

and clear, a beautiful shimmering midnight blue, dressed out in stars of every shade. I floated contentedly on my back, breathing deep fragrant breaths of scented air. I rocked, a child in a golden cradle, awash in rainbow points of brilliant light, turning my head from this side to that, the better to admire it.

CHAPTER EIGHT

Recovery

Moo and I were in Beckenham hospital for several weeks. Moo was the first to recover. She had suffered three broken ribs, a smashed knee and seriously bad bruising to her abdomen and intestines which, more than the other injuries, took a long time to mend after she returned home. I had broken my nose, collar bone, hip and ankle on the left side, punctured the right kidney; and the brick and plaster dust, filled with mouldy spores, had damaged my lungs. On top of that I was experiencing some frightening nightmares and inner fears, which in those days were not really addressed in the way they are in the 21st century, with varying shades of PTSD. It was recognised that, considering my asthma problems, the experience had been all the more traumatic. Moo and I had had a frightening and painful experience but we had survived it. We were, I dare say they'd have said, 'managing to deal with the aftermath in our own ways', and that was all that was important. The fact that whenever I heard that awful deep bubbly growl of a passing Doodle Bug, the sound made me cower under the bed clothes in my hospital bed, feeling faint with fear was, they felt, to be expected. I'd get over it in time. And in time I did get over it – except for now and then, and for many years later, if I heard the sound of a wartime siren in a film I would become quite breathless.[14]

In the first days, Moo was inclined to be tearful and although I was then wired up to the oxygen supply and could not get out of bed, I would stretch my good arm out to her and eventually she would reach out and take it – and the contact seemed to be good for both of us. As the days went by, the nursing staff were watchful and responsive, and we began to improve, until Pa first came to see us and told us that Nesta had died on that day. We were both utterly bereft to hear this, although Moo must have been wondering why there had been no news of her – and I simply was in another place but the loss of Nesta was my first confrontation with death. It was not the fact that I would never see her again, because all partings are made of that sadness, but I was deeply shattered to *know* what she might have gone through before death released her - because I had been there, and it had not released me. For a time, her possible suffering

---

[14] It was a real shock in 1962, on seeing that great film about D-Day, The Longest Day, I had to grip the sides of my cinema seat to stop ducking under it for protection when, eighteen years after the event, that all-too familiar sound of the passing Doodle Bug in the film brought the whole mind-bending experience back into focus for a few moments. To this day, I absolutely cannot manage the Underground, either in London or anywhere else either. My friend Don Jordan persuaded me to use the Underground Metro in Madrid when we spent a week there in 2013, and I nearly passed out – and that was sixty one years after this experience of being buried alive. Some things remain with you and become part of you forever. [DV]

became mine until it occurred to me (possibly Ian's input?) that death might have been instantaneous and she would not have known a thing about it. I held onto that and began to see things in a better light.

Junie was given day leave to come and see us once Moo and I were making good progress and after she had gone, Moo had been very worried to see that beautiful face looking so drawn and strained. She clung to whichever parts of us both were not bandaged or bruised and seemed to have little to say, apart from her relief to be there with us. When details of our experience were brought up in the conversation, she dissolved into floods of tears and Moo said later that, holding Junie's hand, she could feel her trembling all over. She finally departed to get her train back to Bletchley, leaving Moo very troubled at the way Junie was reacting to the whole situation.

"It's not as though we died." She kept saying. "You'd think she was grieving for us, not giving thanks for our lives being spared." I lay in my bed, going over all that we had talked about during Junie's visit – and the subjects that we had not discussed. It came to me that Junie's own life had scarcely been touched-upon, and that she had veered away from it when Moo asked how she was getting on since her arrival at Bletchley a couple of weeks before. We knew all about the Official Secrets Act that they had had to sign. Maybe it had something to do with that. In the end, we decided that our 'near-miss' had been an immense shock to Junie, made all the more frightening by the death of Nesta. Moo decided to discuss Junie with Pa next time he came to see.

Recovery

We must have been in hospital for about three or four weeks, maybe more. It was a great surprise that Pa, having got over his tearful reunion with us, when he sat between our beds and held each of our hands so tightly that Moo had to ask him to let go, eventually took himself in hand and became a hive of activity and decisiveness. He wrote to Moo each day because we could not connect on the telephone, but he was clearly determined to give us all the support that he could muster. By the time we were discharged he had found a flat for us all in a large country house, about nine miles from Bletchley Park. The flat was one of three available in the East wing at Thornton Hall on the Ministry of Defence list of staff accommodation within a ten-mile radius of Bletchley, and there was already a Bletchley scientist staying there.

Pa was very enthusiastic about the Thornton flat because it was owned by the aunt of someone he had known years before, while serving with The Grenadier Guards. Ferrars Loftus had been a fellow subaltern and the young Alan and Ferrars had seen early service together during the Flanders Campaign, which became part of the Battle for Ypres – or 'Wipers,' as it was called in 'Barrack Talk'. I'm pretty sure they did not stay in touch after that period, but Pa was astonished to hear the quite unusual name of Loftus mentioned when going into greater detail about the Harris family who owned Thornton Hall. On closer investigation he discovered that the nephew of Mrs. Harris was indeed the Ferrars Patrick Loftus of their youth, and Pa managed to track him down, discovering that he had married (Betty) in 1925, had a son and daughter of my age, and lived about eight miles away, on the other side of Buckingham.

I was soon wobbling round the ward on crutches and trying not to think how badly the left crutch was hurting my shoulders every time I put any weight on it. I was seriously keen to be allowed to play games at wherever I was next sent to school, having really enjoyed both Lacrosse and Gym at St. Helen's. Moo was still determined that I was to become the next Eileen Joyce – but I was equally determined that I would *not* be! *Impasse!*

Moo and I seem to have become a great deal closer while we were in hospital. I think we were too weak, tackling our various problems, to do anything other than be thoughtful and caring of each other. I was in heaven, of course, because this was the first time that I had had Moo's total attention since infancy, and she seemed so concerned about my well-being and I about hers, that there were no sharp words. I think we must have been star patients as I only recall a good feeling in that place with kindly nurses and wise doctors. It became very important for me to keep Moo's lighter side intact because I do not think I could have borne to face the sharper edge of her tongue at that time. More than likely I was in a fairly fragile state myself, both mentally and physically, even though I was not aware of it.

When Moo was fit to be discharged the doctors felt that I was still in need of their help, but I was quite paranoid about being parted from her and left on my own in a hospital ward while she disappeared to goodness knows where. I must have kicked up quite a scene because eventually I was reluctantly permitted to be discharged with her.

Recovery

I cannot remember anything about the journey until the car drove up a steep hill and turned left in to a long drive between open sloping fields and low hedges. Pa had come with a military staff car to pick us up and bring us back to family life again. The drive must have been almost a quarter of a mile long and its earthy surface was so filled with pot-holes that both Moo and I yelped and gasped our way over that awful surface and arrived at the Front door of Thornton Hall with tears in our eyes and bitten lips!

The Thornton Hall that exists today is very different from the stark and windswept Georgian mansion we first saw, built at the top of a hill so that there were no trees around it, apart from some stubby fruit trees and bushes that cowered to one side.[15] Every passing wind caught and buffeted the structure so that the windows rattled and whistled on the North side and in winter it was a very cold place. The whole building was in two wings in the shape of an L, with the main section facing north and south and the shorter wing facing east and west. It was built of warm red brick but because of its position, there was at that time no creeper growing up its North face, leaving the whole of that side institutionally stark and altogether rather gaunt and

---

[15] When Maudie married Colonel Harris, she found the Old Hall damp, unsuitable to raising children. Colonel Harris, with hundreds of acres to choose from, obligingly agreed to the move. He initially leased the Hall to the Catholic Order of the Sisters of Jesus and Mary at the beginning of the first world war, before he was sent to the Front in France, but in 1917 he let it go completely and the nuns bought the Old Thornton Hall outright from him, renaming it The Convent of Jesus and Mary. Henry meanwhile transferred the name of Thornton Hall to another of his properties on the Thornton estate, which I think had originally been Thornton Manor and farm, as most of it was built in the 17th century, with additions in the 18th and 20th.[DV]

forbidding. Moo pulled a long face at me that was not
entirely to do with pain as we slowly eased ourselves out
of the car and Pa went across to the front door and rang
the bell.

This whole day left an image of great clarity and I dare
say that it is because this place was in such total contrast
to what had happened to us so recently and where we
had been trying to live before. It appeared to be floating
in another period of time, untouched by War, though we
soon discovered that this was not the case. We were
welcomed by a smiling maid and ushered into the hall,
and then through to meet the owner, Mrs. Harris
(Maudie), in the drawing room. The hall was long and
dark, despite having windows either side of the front
door. There were doors to the left (to the dining room)
and right (to the drawing room) and a wide staircase
ahead. The right side of the hall seemed to be closed off
with huge dark blue velvet curtains. The drawing room
was a much more friendly place altogether, light and
bright and filled with flowers and the scent of roses, and
the woman who rose from her chair to greet us was
elderly but still had the structure of youthful beauty in
her face. It was a charming, dignified face, its faint lines,
set in sadness, deepening into laughter when she spoke,
reflecting traces of an old mischief which seemed never
quite erased. Moo, Pa and I were made comfortable in
Mrs. Harris's drawing room and tea was brought, which
we drank with great delight, having suffered the doubtful
benefits of stewed tea *a la* hospital tea urn for the last
month or so. Here we spent half an hour eating freshly
baked small but delicious rock cakes, washed down with
the delicate aromatic flavours of a mixture of Assam and
fragrant China teas, drunk from fine porcelain rather
than stout white canteen cups.

We were questioned about our narrow escape until it was clear that we were both still in a degree of shock over the whole event, at which point she tactfully switched to telling us about herself and her family. Colonel Harris had only died a few months before in 1943 and she was still trying to come to terms with the recent death in action of her only son Francis, (always known as Boy) in February of this very year of 1944. She spoke very simply and one could see that those fine lines had not been in her face until recently but the death of both the adored men in her life, so close together, had really been a very heavy blow. She was, however, born a Bolton – and in Victorian times, women in particular were trained to steel themselves with courage in the face of any disaster. When I grew to know the family better, it was always astonishing that this youngest child of the Bolton family, so petted and spoiled by everyone for her sunny nature and bright beauty, would have it in her to not only survive the worst double loss of her whole life with such dignity but she was also capable of filling the room with laughter.[16] Listening to that quiet sad but

---

[16] One of the more obvious proofs of Maudie's mischievous and sometimes wilful nature remains for all to see today. When her husband died in 1943, the nuns were keen for her to put up a suitably dignified headstone, because the hamlet's tiny parish church is not only in the school grounds but stands across the wide graveled entrance sweep, immediately opposite the main front door of Thornton College. [see pic] Maudie was incensed that the nuns appeared to be giving her directions of how her husband should or should not have his headstone – and the monument she erected over her husband's grave is an almost life-sized and very naked image in bronze of the pagan Mercury, Roman messenger of the gods. You will find the Harris Mercury proudly standing on one leg on his fine Portland stone plinth, with his dangly bits in very prominent view over the grave, which also now embraces the remains of Maudie herself, and both Boy and Nina. Looking a little closer into why Maudie might have chosen Mercury to annoy the nuns, rather than any of the many other more respectable Greek or Roman gods, I can only guess that since Mercury was the God of Desire as well as

hopeful voice was very good for both Moo and me. It made us stop thinking of ourselves just then and showed us very clearly why Junie especially had been so utterly devastated when she heard what had befallen us.

22 - Two "Bolton sisters" - Maudie (Mrs. Harris) on the left and Alice (Grandma Loftus) on the right

After tea, the elderly housekeeper took us upstairs to the flat on the East side of the house. That day, she took us up the main staircase and through a connecting door to what must have once been the staff corridor, with more modest bedrooms and maybe the housekeeper's rooms. There were two double bedrooms, the smaller one opening from the larger one and both had windows facing south. They overlooked a delightful sunken rose garden and paths to distant hedges, behind which were

---

Commerce, it was her way of celebrating Colonel Harris's success not only with his splendid brand of pies and sausages, but also his excellence as a partner. Fortunately for the nuns at Thornton I am relieved to observe that even Maudie would not have had the courage to give her Mercury the three phalluses that were found on a Mercury statue discovered in Tongeren, Belgium. Her message was and still is however, quite clear![DV]

the vegetable gardens, greenhouses and beyond that the farm buildings. There was a bathroom, which we would share with the other Bletchley Park scientist, Hugh Creighton, who also had a bedroom, sitting room and small kitchen up on the first floor. A narrow, typical 'back' stairway let down to the ground floor and a passage with doors left and right off it, where we discovered a nice light north-facing kitchen which was next to the main house kitchens, a downstairs lavatory, and on the south side again, a cosy sitting room for us to use which had a French window opening out onto the garden. There was a door at the end of the passage which accessed a small courtyard, and this was the entrance that we were asked to use, rather than going through the main house. It was a bit higgledy-piggledy – but it was somewhere to lay our heads, and it was as far away from the war-torn pressures of Southern and Eastern England as we had ever been. Moo sat on a chair in the bedroom that she and Pa would share, and allowed a tear to trickle down her nose. I put my good arm round her, and she said to Pa as he patted her cheek in the way he always did.

"It's all right. I'm just so happy to be here, Darling. It's such a relief......" and it was. This great redbrick house standing proudly at the top of its hill, under a near-cloudless summer sky felt so safe, so undisturbed by history and time. Its windows spanned the soft greens and yellows of a beautiful Buckinghamshire landscape of farmland, woods and a glint of the river Ouse in the distance below; it all seemed like a dream-sequence when our heads had been filled for so long with the sights and sounds of destruction and death. Maybe it had not even occurred to either of us before that moment, that everyone within striking distance of the

War was now so accustomed to danger, deprivation and waiting for the next Alert that we had forgotten how it felt to be safe – to relax and not to have to be brave but purely enjoy – both the surroundings and the company of those who had hardly been touched by the demons that had been haunting our lives.

I do not remember how that first day finished. I know I was very tired and because of the various damaged parts, did not have the energy to go and explore. I do know that later that evening I watched Pa busying himself with getting us some supper, which was an amazing sight because Pa always regarded the kitchen as a foreign land, and was not, as far as I could remember, even able to boil a kettle. Now he pottered between the kitchen – where the Harrises had kindly stocked the larder with enough food for us to manage until we could get to some shops - a look of complete happiness on his face as he brought in a tray with bowls of steaming soup and hunks of fresh bread piled on a large plate. There were rather battered tin spoons to scoop up our soup with, and some very old knives with worn bone handles but it didn't matter. We were here together at last and maybe we could stay that way for long enough to get ourselves back to full strength and health.

"Why isn't Junie here?" I finally asked Pa, having tried not to ever since we had arrived and she had not been there to greet us. "She's on duty." He said right away. "I think she said she's coming over tomorrow but she is not very communicative at the moment so I'll phone through to her section at six o'clock to see what the situation is."

Moo had drowsed off after enjoying the warmth and freshness of the vegetable soup, but she opened her eyes and looked around her, and then said, "I'll go upstairs and see about putting our things away. I'll have to make a list of what we need from the shops because we have nothing, Alan …. nothing at all, apart from the hand-me-downs the hospital gave us." I didn't think that this situation had crossed Pa's mind but he patted his pockets, tutting to himself, until he found an envelope.

"Oh dear, I forgot all about this. I was given this to pass on to you so that you can get yourselves kitted out tomorrow. Mrs. Harris's daughter, Nina Young, has offered to take you into Buckingham to do some shopping in the morning. There's money here, and emergency ration cards. When you are feeling stronger, you have to go into the Civil Defence office to get another lot of gas masks for yourselves, but I dare say that can wait. This is for clothes and food."

Moo looked relieved. I think she imagined that Pa, with his mind on his job, was simply not up to thinking ahead for this kind of emergency – and it was miraculous to discover that, in fact, he seemed to have thought of everything.

*

I only have a vague memory of the days that followed our arrival at Thornton. The Buckingham doctor, John Bostock, who eventually became a long-term family friend, came out to examine us both, bringing the district nurse with him, because we had dressings to be changed and our various problems to be registered. There was such kindness all around us. We met Nina Young who lived with her three little girls in the West wing of the house and whose husband Major John Young was still away on War service. I do not know much about him, although I do remember the day he returned from the Front. He had been away for over a year then; and Nina's excitement and terrible nervousness was shared by us all, and I remember the new pink and navy blue dress she had had made to wear when she greeted him.

Within two days of our arrival at Thornton Hall, Bletchley Park phoned Moo to tell her that Junie was in the Sanitorium, suffering from exhaustion. The following day she was moved to Bletchley hospital. Pa phoned in great distress to say that the doctors had decided that Junie was having a nervous breakdown. This was a real shock to us, but sadly it was not a shock to Bletchley Park, as there was by this time a steady number of young women operators of the de-coding equipment who cracked and collapsed under the moment-by-moment strain of tackling the complications of de-coding German Enigma messages.

Junie had begun to operate the Bombe machine while she had been stationed at Eastcote at HMS Pembroke, but she had then moved to Bletchley where she found the stress of any mistake her end, possibly resulting in the deaths of our servicemen elsewhere, became an unbearable worry. The last straw was when she heard that we had been hit by a flying bomb and that Moo and I were initially presumed killed. Junie and Pa had not been brought up-to-date five hours later when we were located, but some twelve hours later when we had actually been admitted to hospital. It was too much for her and she began to see things that were not there and to complain of terrible headaches. Eventually she fainted during a work period – and her state of mind was at last noticed.

23 - Like so many young Wrens at Bletchley Park in 1943, Junie (bottom left) was traumatised by the work she was doing - but she had almost lost her family and the combined shock was too much for her

Moo and I steadily improved, bodies healing, and I eventually stopped having dreams about being suffocated. Moo – had been down to the village to visit the convent at the old Thornton Hall, and the nuns had agreed to take me into the school as a day girl for the coming September term, although I would be the only one as, at that time, all the other children were boarders.

The first day of term at Thornton College was quite strange because all the children had arrived the previous day and, hobbling into the school hall with my trusty stick, I was viewed with some curiosity, especially when it became known that I was living up the hill and would be walking the 1.5 miles to school and back every day. This was nothing out of the usual in those days where we all did a lot more walking, but though I had long abandoned the crutch, I still needed the support of my walking stick, and walking down the long hill from the

House to the school was at first a painful experience, only fractionally less painful than walking back up the hill at the end of the school day. The school was a mile and a quarter from the gate of Thornton Hall – but the pot-holed drive was almost another quarter mile on top of that. I stuck to it grimly for the first two weeks, sometimes arriving at school soaked to the skin – which also happened going home, but that was not so bad because I could always have a nice rub-down in front of the fire. At school I had to have a complete change of clothes so that eventually Reverend Mother Gonzaga (whose secular Spanish name had been, rather romantically 'Alveira Boutele') persuaded Moo to let me borrow a bicycle for the rest of the term. I was quite keen on this, despite the continuing trouble with my shoulders, having learned to ride a bike with Guy and Christopher Fernau. With the help of a bike at Thornton, and my stick strapped on my back, I could fairly whizzzz down the long lane into the village soon after eight every school morning, and be in Assembly by the time roll-call and morning prayers were said. It was not so good returning home in the evening. I had to push it all the way up the hill and was only able to set off on two wheels again once I had staggered through the gate. Despite the aches and pains, I quite enjoyed the drive to the house with all its holes and half-hidden boulders because it all became a game of how I could stay on the saddle, while avoiding the deep and muddy puddles and certain lethal stones that were hiding, ready to unseat me. I am pretty sure I never did actually fall off that bike because my body was still healing and would have fallen apart again had I inflicted any more damage to it.

Junie had been away in some sort of nursing home for about six weeks and by the time she was allowed to return to us for a period of sick leave at Thornton, she was a shadow of her former self, thin and pale with grey smudges under those lovely violet eyes that gave her a haunted look. She and I shared the second bedroom and although at first I was delighted for her to be there with me, I soon found that she did not want to talk; there was no sign of the old camaraderie of years gone past when we often shared a room, and always had marvellous discussions about everything from the size of the Solar System to what her children would be called when she was married. Now that comfortable intimacy seemed to have disappeared and she would spend a lot of the day on her bed, either pretending to read or simply gazing into space. When I tried to chat with her she told me shortly to 'shut up because she had a headache.' I drew away and began to resent her presence in what was, after all, my bedroom.

"You have to be patient," Moo said when I complained about being shut out of my own room. "She has been under a lot of mental strain and the doctors say that only time and understanding will solve the problem." So I left Junie to her sad dreaming, said nothing about Moo's and my own damaged bodies and minds which were still not fully healed, and switched my thoughts to making new friends at Thornton college.

During the first term at the college I was carefully assessed. My French was by this time almost forgotten because I had not used it, not even heard it used for four years, but I still had the correct pronunciation so it was assumed that I was fluent in the language. I suffered from poor marks when it was realised that my writing of

French was almost nil and my vocabulary threadbare. They quickly discovered that where Maths was concerned, I was a complete non-starter. Bottom in Arithmetic, Algebra, and Geometry. Pretty close to the bottom for Geography and only middling for History. However, where Art, all English subjects and singing were concerned I was in good order with my teachers. My only sadness was that Moo once again quickly dashed my hopes – and when the other girls were playing tennis and lacrosse, I was having piano practice. However, all was not lost because, once I was able to run and behave normally again, I was allowed to play Lacrosse, although at first I had to be goalie, where I would not be required to rush about and get hit by passing Lax sticks. I absolutely *loved* Lacrosse and became quite nippy on my feet as time went by.

Because of what had happened to Moo and me, I discovered that I was feeling rather quiet and pensive at school, which had little to do with being a new girl. The argumentative streak seems to have gone out of me and, in no time, I made friends with both the children and the nuns. At first they had wanted to hear all about my 'horrible experience' but it was soon apparent that I simply could not talk about it and the nuns (I was later told) warned the girls not to question me as I had gone through a terrible episode and needed time to get over it. The subject was not mentioned again and, to my relief, I was soon to settle into a comfortable and satisfying routine. Even the painful uphill bike-pushing in all weathers did not bother me much after a time, though Moo, on the road to recovery herself, at last began to notice how breathless I always was by the time I reached the house.[17]

*

Halfway through my first term I had met Heather Loftus and become firm friends in a group of about five or six girls, and I do not think I had ever been happier at any of the schools that had suffered me. Moo and Pa seemed much happier with me too. There had not been a single complaint about unruly behaviour, indeed the nuns Moo talked to concerning my indifferent school-work were mostly very encouraging, and several of them expressed actual approval. Mrs. Harris decided, as early wet weather closed in and getting to our distant side entrance just made us all even wetter, that we should use the main front door and get to our quarters through her dining room. In this way, we sometimes met in the hall and she would always ask how I was enjoying the convent. On my fourteenth birthday, when we had only been in the flat for a few weeks, she called me into her drawing room and gave me a delightful pair of little porcelain French poodles, which I still have. My instant devotion to her enormous but elderly Airedale, Robbie, had not escaped her attention and the way that Robbie returned my affection suggested that I might prove to be quite an agreeable child. She knew that I was to enjoy a birthday tea party later that evening, which included the two elder Young girls, and Pa was bringing Hugh Creighton in for a drink later on, but she wanted to give

---

[17] Moo paid another visit to the convent during my second term at Thornton – and by the time the Summer term arrived it had been decided that, come the next school year, the September term, I was to become a weekly boarder, staying home at weekends and sleeping at school during the week [DV]

me her little gift personally, apparently to let me know that she was also aware that I had become friends at school with her great-niece Heather Loftus.

Heather had a great love of horses and that commitment stayed with her for her entire life. I had not had much to do with horses in my transient life, even though I had begun to ride when we were at Batchworth Heath and Moo had arranged, during those summer holidays, for me to have riding lessons twice a week for the whole eight weeks. So I was attracted by the way she rode her horses, what she did with them – and how devotedly she looked after them, particularly her own beloved pony *Brownie*.

Heather was also mad about American jazz and when she invited me to stay at Tingewick Hall, where the Loftuses lived several miles the other side of Buckingham, we listened to the American Forces Network every night, when we should have been asleep in bed. After my first term at Thornton, we wrote to each other throughout the holidays, and because of the paper shortage, used sticky labels on the same envelope on which to write our addresses. Eventually, the envelope became so bulky with layer upon layer of labels that we had to pay extra for the letters and Moo put a stop to this little game. Heather had a great passion of buying American magazines when they began to appear in the shops, in order to get all the gossip on the film stars and musicians. This kind of 'gossip reporting' was becoming more and more the way we in Britain were being entertained and cheered up as the Nation's bankrupt economy ate into our everyday lives. Sometimes she would come across a new and original idea for decorating Brownie's mane, or become besotted with some particular jazz number. As we were allowed to play our own records during mid-morning 'break' and in the evenings, I soon got used to Heather's latest passions. The tune she constantly played that first term at Thornton was Benny Goodman with a very young Peggy Lee singing "Why Don't You Do Right By Me?" (*Get outa here – and get me some money tooooo*). As I had been brought up on classical music and then the lovely songs of Richard Tauber and the charming British musicals of composers like Vivian Ellis, Noel Coward and Ivor Novello, I had never really listened to American music on the wireless. However, once Heather started me off, I became fascinated by the music of American composers such as Jerome Kern, Irving Berlin, and my favourite Cole Porter. I still love the beautiful music and lyrics of these 20th century composers. Of course, Heather was much more interested in Dixieland jazz from people like Jelly Roll Morton and Cab Calloway, but although I enjoyed that infectious 'beat', I found I preferred the more romantic elements – maybe the memory of Guy Fernau was still in the back of my mind. Both Guy and Christopher wrote to me at Thornton but after a year or so we lost touch. I suppose I have tended to prefer light music by composers such as Cole Porter because they are always so wonderful to sing – and that is where my preference always lay. Having said that, Heather's American jazz introduced me to various superb piano players and when she put on a record by Count Basie, Dave Brubeck, Art Tatum or Oscar Petersen I was transfixed and wondered if I'd be allowed to try my hand at such wonderful, rolling FREE-flowing sound. That idea was very quickly flattened. I was definitely not permitted to waste my time trying to improvise, *a la* Brubeck, and Moo showed signs of returning to her former strictness and irritation with me when the subject was raised. I did not mention it again, realising that I could, if Heather continued to invite me over to stay, have a quiet tinkle on the ivories at Tingewick, as there was a grand piano there – and Heather's brother Geoff, who was a gifted pianist, had indicated that he would be happy to teach me a few bars of the more modern stuff, if I was interested. And I certainly was. What a joy it would be, not to have to practice only my scales, arpeggios and exam pieces – and just float away on some glorious ripple of sound to which I could also sing. Life was definitely beginning to look up.

During that first stay at Tingewick, I was immediately struck by its homeliness, how it embraced me but there was also a fire about Tingewick. The Loftus family were dazzling, larger than life, they didn't judge me, made no demands on me just accepted me for who I was, which was a welcome relief from the austerity and strictures of my own family. I had been given the second bed in Heather's room and we had talked almost all night and then had difficulty getting up in the morning.

Heather and I went to the stables the next day to groom her pony Brownie and the much larger horse - Fusilier, who her father Ferrars was a little afraid of. Moo had said that I couldn't ride until after my shoulder had healed, so we spent the morning side by side, mucking out and filling their nose bags. Heather's main occupation was grooming and riding the two horses and the mounts of several of her friends. She seemed quite unconcerned that I had no riding experience and the fact that all hunting, racing and stable talk went straight over my head. One weekend at Tingewick, I complained about not riding when Heather flew into the saddle on Fusilier as I held his bridle "Never mind." She said blithely. "Just wait until your shoulder is mended, then we'll get you out on Brownie and you'll be riding Fusilier in no time and be as madly in love with them as I am."

And, in all truth, I was longing to ride, longing to feel as easy in the saddle as I felt helping Heather with the stable chores. Geoff came back from school that weekend with a clutter of trunks and sports gear. We eyed each other cautiously and kept our distance. He plunged into the stripping down of the engine of his pride and joy, an old "Chummy" Austin and groaned about having' two ruddy girls to contend with now, when one was bad enough already' and Heather retorted that we were far too busy to either bother him or be bothered with him so he could drown in sump oil for all she cared.

24 - Geoff also liked to fly (Stowe School)

He became a pair of oily feet sticking out from under his car, a string of dis-embodied curses and, at the dinner table, a streakily scrubbed beanpole with blond hair plastered damply to his head and smelling of an unnatural compound of his father's Bay Rum hair tonic, liberally mixed with Castrol. We lounged about in the drawing room, listening to Charlie Kuntz's piano playing or Hoagey Carmichael singing in that quirky, sandpapery voice of his and sometimes we would join in the funny, gimmicky songs which were cheering up our Forces all over the world, songs with zany words and titles like 'Chattanooga Choo Choo' and 'Mairzy Doats and Dozy Doats' yelled happily at the tops of our voices until someone hammered on the door to tell us to reduce the din.

I exercised my shoulder with great determination, once it was free of the plaster, because there was nothing I wanted to do more than ride Brownie with Heather. Meanwhile, I had to be content with hanging around the stables, giving a hand with the mash, stuffing the hay bags with the stable lad, or wandering across the yard to the garage block where a perspiring but happy Geoff now had his engine out on blocks and was stripping it down. I learned about gaskets, tappets and fuel injection - until a school friend of Geoffs' arrived to spend a week and abruptly I ceased to exist. As luck would have it, the doctor decided that I might do a little gentle riding, by then, and so my tuition began and there was no time for cars for the rest of that holidays.

I found, much to my surprise, that, apart from the lingering stiffness in my shoulder, I was very comfortable on Brownie. We seemed to move naturally together, without nervousness – after I had got over the strangeness of sitting astride the warm creaking saddle for the first time. Heather was endlessly patient, showing me how to hold the reins, where to grip with my knees, the angle my feet should be in the stirrups.

"You should teach horsemanship when you leave school." I suggested, constantly impressed with the dogged way she made me practice again and again until I was moving and controlling my mount naturally. She grinned at me.

"You don't think I'd waste my wonderful youth on dim heads, do you? I just want you to be able to keep up with me so that we can really have a bit of fun. I'm going to train eventually, I suppose - and do as much point-to-pointing as I can in the meantime. We'll do it together." And we did – before long, we were riding the eight miles between Tingewick and Thornton, which just meant that I spent more time at Tingewick.

*

Just before my fourteenth birthday that October, the War had taken several positive and a few negative turns. The British Army returned to Greece and liberated its capital, Athens, but closer to home, earlier victories in gaining a foothold in Normandy were not going so well and Germany over-ran and took Arnhem, in the Netherlands, securing this key point from British paratroopers who had dropped in to defend Arnhem's bridge over the river Rhine.

Everyone in the school was now focused closely on what was happening on the Allies' various sectors of War, which seemed to stretch all round the World, owing to the War in the Far East with Japan. This

185

conflict between Japan, the Allies and America had hardly been noticed by civilians in Britain until the attack on Pearl Harbour in December 1941 had brought the United States a few months later tumbling into the fray. This was followed by a great defeat for Britain in the Far East when the Japanese marched the length of Malaya and took Singapore, a British colony – whose guns had apparently been trained out to sea at the time. Whatever the circumstances, it was a cause of great dismay and shame to Britain, and from it began the long struggle that was to be called 'The Burma Campaign' and which was fought from January 1942 to July 1945. Because it was so far away from The United Kingdom and because our attention was naturally focused on what was going on close to our own doorstep, the dreadful conditions under which our Army, Navy and Air forces and their allies fought were hardly appreciated. It was not until well after all these wars were over that the photographs of war correspondents and the sketches of war artists were published and the full horror of that terrible situation was finally understood. So there were three separate sectors of War to keep an eye on, and in which everyone had fathers, brothers and sons, and even some daughters. It is quite astonishing, on reflection, the way the British population managed to keep up their determined good cheer when death and destruction was going on all round us. How can one do anything but sympathise with those who were at the forefront of War, and found the pressure and horror just too much to bear? But there was also the home front. As a very young teenager, I did not understand Junie's shattered mind at the time she was in that state, or even for some time afterwards. All I saw was this silent, white-faced, even *haggard* Junie who would not talk to me and who would turn away whenever I wanted to give her comfort. Junie's 'headaches' became a sad and cutting-off part of life – and would continue to be used as an excuse for non-communication forever after.

I was also, aged fourteen, quite unaware of Pa's occupation, except that he was involved with things to do with radio and complicated new technological equipment. But I think it might have been at this time that Moo let slip the occasional fact that Pa had, when we were in London and then when I was at Shiplake, been dropped several times by parachute into France to set up wireless 'cells' so that the Maquis (the French Resistance organisation) could maintain contact with the Free French in England. It explained why Pa had arrived home on one occasion looking as though he had been in a fight, and had simply said that he had fallen out of a tree. As I have already related, we had assumed that this was his way of saying 'I cannot tell you the reason' and had accepted it as such – but I gradually came to understand that my dear old Pa, by that time fifty years of age and much too elderly for parachute jumps in those days, had been dropping into France whenever he was required to do so. It was never clear how many drops he had done. I think there were three but Junie, years later said he had done five before anyone realised that this was a younger man's responsibility. Certainly he suffered, sometimes quite badly, from aches and pains in his hips and a shoulder for the rest of his life. I never ever heard him complain. Pa's age may well have saved his life at this time, because, just before Christmas in 1944 he came home with a very nifty greatcoat with a high collar, and a bag of other cold-weather clothing. There was a lot of quiet conversation between him and Moo, whose face then assumed one of her looks that boded ill for someone. That someone must have been Pa's commanding officer as she wore that grimly determined expression for a week. It cleared miraculously one day, not long afterwards when Pa came home with a spring in his step to tell her that his trip was now OFF. It seems that there had been a move afoot to send him on a drop into Germany, since his German was so perfect, to an area close to Peenemunde, where the V2s were being built and launched. Just how they would have expected him to invade an island on his own and then be able to find his way back through a sector of fierce fighting, bombing and destruction, history does not relate. We always felt those in command had been willing to sacrifice Pa's life without a qualm on a mere whim – an elderly ex-soldier of no great value – and not even to the greater good. Whatever Moo said to his CO seemed to do the trick though and, in any case, shortly after that it became apparent that the Germans were setting up a whole swathe of 'portable' launching sites across Northern Germany and into Holland – and there was no longer a need for him to go, after one of the sites was taken by allied forces. Pa kept the long greatcoat and wore it every winter, looking like a Polish general with its high collar and solid grey wool tweed.

I had two Christmases in 1944. One was shared with Mrs. Harris and the Youngs and then Heather invited me over to Tingewick where New Year was celebrated with the lifting of many glasses and I had my first taste of Whisky. I thought it was disgusting. However, Geoff and Heather had all kinds of interesting flavours to add to it and, having tried soda, orange bitters, and angostura, I finally decided that it wasn't too bad with ginger ale. Goodness knows what was on our menu for

Christmas and New Year in 1944. We would, of course, have had turkey because they were naturally reared in the United Kingdom in wartime as well as in peacetime, and have been ever since we had caught the Turkey-eating habit at Christmas from the USA. I do recall that the Home Farm at Thornton reared a small 'raft' of turkeys especially for the Hall's Christmas table, and no doubt the tables of the Estate staff too. We would have had fresh vegetables, apple stuffing and possibly a little bacon from our rations. The Christmas pudding would not have had the dried fruit we know today but I remember us going through all kinds of clever ways to dry or marinade cherries, plums and other home-grown 'berry' fruits in order to have some sort of replacement for the dates, sultanas and raisins that were no longer available. Our hunted and hounded merchant ships had to concentrate on transporting essential supplies that were necessary for our everyday lives. Oranges and lemons, bananas and pineapples were wonders that a whole generation of children had only seen in picture books and so we compromised and used whatever we had available, and we dried black and red currants, and all the other berries and they seemed to do nearly as well.

We made all our own Christmas presents, cards and decorations, which ensured that preparing for Christmas was all the more fun. Goodness knows what we made and gave each other that Christmas but I do know that Heather made me a very decorative eye patch to wear, since one of my battle scars was a deep cut over my left eyebrow which had still not healed properly and I think I was probably a bit sensitive about it! The eye patch was a beautiful yellow sunflower with a big blue eye in the centre. I wore it with pride, probably because Geoff seemed to find it rather attractive!

Our own Christmas was very quiet because Junie simply could not take too much chatter. She was very slowly improving but was still inclined to leave the table or the room without warning, maybe if I was being argumentative or Moo was telling us all what we should or should not be doing. Sometimes it would be if Hugh Creighton joined us for a meal. For some reason, Junie seemed to avoid Hugh who was actually so shy that he would never have tried to become too familiar with her. She was, of course, already beginning to protect herself from the often-cloying admiration and intrusiveness of the opposite sex, who all saw her as stunningly beautiful and appealing, and so all her admirers wanted to know her better, and you may be sure that they did not want to have deep intellectual conversations. She gradually learned how to cope with this never-ending situation, but in 1944 she had lost all her defences and would simply collapse if anyone tried to insist on anything at all. It was, dare I say it, a relief when Heather and Geoff came over and drove me back to spend the New Year with them. This must have been the time when I first came to know their home at Tingewick, and I started to create quiet, almost mantra moments, and took myself off to bed in my small room next to one referred to by Heather as 'Nanny's', at the end of the bedroom corridor. I was growing up - I could feel the difference and it had gradually become important to take a look at what I was intending to grow up into. I know I thought about our family's situation a lot and could see myself being whisked back to Switzerland after the War and never seeing my friends again. I still exchanged regular letters with Bridget Forbes, the friend from my Batchworth Heath days, it was possible that the Furnaus might want to keep in touch with me, and now I had a whole raft of new friends at Thornton College, of which the Loftus and Bolton cousins were presently at the top of my list. I did not want to lose any of them, so I had to think of an occupation that would keep me in England, that Moo would not dismiss out of hand.

CHAPTER NINE

New Hope – VE Day

I think this is a good moment to give you a more complete picture of what Tingewick Hall was like,[18] including the personalities of the family who lived there and gave me that unexpected sense of serene stability

---

[18] The house was not a great mansion but a comfortable and gracious house with three reception rooms around a wide hall downstairs, and an extensive kitchen wing containing the servants hall, butler's pantry, two large kitchens and a long cold larder. Upstairs on the first floor there were four double bedrooms, three bathrooms, two nurseries, and three staff rooms. On the top attic floor were two more staff rooms. Outside, there was an enormous garage for three/four cars, four stables for the horses and two tack rooms. In the grounds there was a gardener's cottage and at the entrance gates a lodge, where one of the staff (Wyn Jones) lived with her husband. [DV]

completely absent from their lives.[19]   Tingewick was filled with music, laughter, dancing and yes, shouting, and it was to become my spiritual home, a very unlikely sanctuary for a troubled young mind recovering from war trauma.

Tingewick Hall was surrounded by a garden and fields covering around six acres, including a beautiful walled kitchen garden, which kept the family going with fresh vegetables and fruit throughout the war. The field at the back of the house served as an occasional airstrip, when Ferrars flew *The Bag* (GA-BAG, his own private Gipsy Moth airplane) in from its regular hanger at Kidlington, a grass runway airfield, northwest of Oxford. As one of the Tingewick fields sported a heavy telephone cable with two small pylons to support it cutting across its centre, take-offs and landings here were always

---

[19] Betty's father, Harold Winterbottom (JP), was High Sheriff of Northamptonshire and one of the wealthiest men in Britain. He had decided on an arranged marriage for his only and much loved daughter to the dashing son of a cricketing friend from the withered branch of an old but penniless aristocratic family on "the shivering verge of gentility". When Ferrars and Betty married in 1925, Harold wanted to give them a lavish property as he had done for his sons before her. They visited a number of sprawling estates with a view to buying including Stowe House (later to become Stowe School – the family still has the sales brochure for Stowe House).[GL] Betty was much more practical, however, and wanted a smaller house she could feel at home in, so they decided upon was an old rectory, no longer in use in the village of Tingewick, three miles from Buckingham on the road to Bicester and Oxford. The house, empty for some years, had to be gutted and completely renovated before it could be lived-in, and so the young couple rented Tingewick House, on the opposite side of the Buckingham to Bicester road in the centre of the village. Geoffrey was actually born in Tingewick House, and the Loftuses moved to the Hall, I think in 1927, and stayed there until Betty's death in 1972. Originally, in the seventeen hundreds, the rectory at Tingewick had been built much further forward in its large plot of land so that it was in line with the church, but around 1854, for some reason, the whole house was pulled down, brick by brick, moved about 50 yards back and rebuilt and the old footings became a rock garden. [DV]

"interesting," to put it mildly. The house itself was built with large windows, and tall chimneys in the Tudor style so that smoke billowing from them would be taken up and dispersed by winds and currents. The rooms were all spacious without being too large, and as they were furnished with charm and a lack of ostentation, the occasional beautiful piece of furniture would be instantly recognised and appreciated. The items that really stood out were two enormous pictures which were hung to the left and right of the wide staircase as it curved up to the first floor from the broad 'T' shaped hall. The wall on the left of the stairs was filled with a huge, over life-sized portrait of an ancestral Loftus, which I irreverently nicknamed Mickey Rooney because that's who it looked like. Glaring stonily across the stair well on the right side of the staircase was a life-sized portrait of Betty's father, Harold Winterbottom, sitting at his desk looking dignified and Edwardian, with neat head and drooping facial hair that all gentlemen wore in those days.

26 - Ferrars Loftus (aged 50) in the uniform of RAFVR (volunteer reserve)

The house was run without fuss by a team who had been with the family since they had arrived in 1927. Mary and Emily Jones, and occasionally their sister-in-law Wyn, who lived with their brother in the Lodge, though Wyn was really the seamstress for the family. Mary and Emily looked after the fabric of the House but lived in a cottage outside the gates, beside the church. The cook was Mabel who did 'live in,' and she had the two rooms at the top of

194

the house. I will tell you more of them as we go along. All of them called me Miss Diney, just as Rose from the Shiplake household had called me.

I think the only 'domestic' chore that Ferrars did, apart from tending the households three cars, was to wind the clocks every Wednesday morning.[20] As there were six clocks downstairs and four upstairs, this was a time-consuming and meticulous business as, in that list, were three exotic and valuable grandfather clocks, all of which had their own unique idiosyncrasies and had to be treated with great respect and plenty of TLC. The internal walls in the rest of the house were lined with Loftus family portraits. Since I was clearly not unduly impressed by all this display of past grandeur, I'm afraid that I gave nicknames to all of the portraits, which Betty found hilarious, and Ferrars tried to be amused but was not.

---

[20] Ferrars Loftus had, at the beginning of the second World War, joined the Royal Air Force, in view of the fact that he not only had a pilot's licence but actually owned a beautiful 1934 Gipsy Moth biplane. It was a frequent joke in the Loftus family that, should there ever be a third World War, Ferrars would certainly join the Royal Navy so that he could claim truthfully to have served his Country in all three Services. Ferrars Loftus was, of course, too old by 1939 to become a fighter pilot in the RAF. Having been born in 1891, he was by then 50 years of age but he was accepted first as a Pilot Officer and later became a Squadron Leader, (ground staff) and throughout the war was posted to various air stations within traveling distance of his home at Tingewick, near Buckingham. [DV]

In the dining room were three wonderful Italianate pastoral scenes in oil, in ornate frames. The house also boasted several display cabinets of beautiful and valuable porcelain, the one Loftus possession that Betty was very fond of. The result was that there were a lot of china cabinets at Tingewick, both downstairs and upstairs. I began to be interested in old porcelain through the devotion for it of Gran Finlay, who would tell Junie and me, when we were very small, all about the evolution of pottery into porcelain and the histories of various makes, but the china at Tingewick cemented that interest.[21]

The Loftus family were pillars of the local community, holding regular fetes and charity events on the grounds at Tingewick, with Ferrars serving as an Inspector of Special Constable for the County and Betty as Master of the Bicester Hunt. Ferrars also served as an officer RAFVR during the war but it was what happened behind closed doors that made Tingewick so compelling. Ferrars and Betty had an open marriage, free to take their pleasures where they found them. Tingewick was the venue for regular weekend house parties, throughout the 1930s, which continued into the War. Early on in my visits to Tingewick, there was much talk about Betty's pre-war 'best friend' Diana Caldwell, and the handsome piano-playing Vernon Motion, who fell in love with each other at Tingewick – each thinking

27 - Betty Loftus circa 1942

---

[21] In later years, Betty would send me valuable pieces by post but never bothered with packaging, so they always arrived smashed. [DV]

the other must be very wealthy. Neither of them was! They were both penniless 'hangers-on' and married in a rush of lust and greed – only to discover their mistake within days.[22]

The household, when I was first introduced to it, was made up of Betty, Ferrars, Geoff and Heather, Nanny Georgie Elliot, and John Arbuthnot, who lived in one of the main guest bedrooms; and Billie Fleck, Ferrars' 'friend' who was a constant weekend visitor to Tingewick. These two extra 'family' members were

---

[22] I make an excursion here for information and context – Diana and Vernon soon parted and Diana, having then met Jock Broughton at Tingewick, went off with him to Kenya, Africa at the beginning of the War and married him as soon as his wife Vera (Boscawen), who had been at school at St. Leonards with Moo, could be persuaded to divorce him. Broughton was, to give him his full title, Sir Henry John (Jock) Delves-Broughton, 11th Baronet. The reason for these details is hardly to impress you, but to relate Tingewick's responsibility for the, by now (in)famous murder in Kenya, which years later resulted in a book and a film called *White Mischief.* Jock Broughton was accused (but acquitted) of the murder of The Earl of Erroll in Kenya in 1941 and committed suicide in 1942. The reason for all this was that Diana, only just married to Jock, was already having a very open affaire with Lord Erroll, despite that dilettante's on-going affaire with another woman, a very rich and fast-living American called Alice de Janze. Jock Broughton, rejected by the notorious Happy Valley set, crept back to England and took his own life while Diana sailed on to the next husband, Gilbert Colville. He was a wealthy and rather reclusive homosexual rancher who owned large tracts of the Great Rift Valley in Kenya and Diana married him in 1943. After little more than a decade, during which time Diana and Gilbert adopted a daughter, Diana reverted to type, divorced Colville and married Lord Delamere, the largest landowner, Chairman of the Kenya Farmers Association and leader of Kenya society. Gilbert must have remained fond of Diana because, being immensely wealthy, he left both his adopted daughter and Diana a huge fortune and thousands of acres of Africa. The Delamere marriage hung together, fortunately, and Diana was still playing The First Lady of Kenya when I started flying in and out of Nairobi in 1960, when I would always visit my parents' friend John Lees and his family at their Muthaiga house. I am still in touch with the two daughters, Susan and Carol (who still lives in Nairobi). Lord Delamere gave up the unequal struggle in 1979. Diana followed him in 1987, outliving her friend and partner-fixer Betty Loftus by nearly a decade. [DV]

understood to be the permanent amoratas of Betty and Ferrars, although there were frequent visits by others who fleetingly held their attention. Betty had a lovely nature, kind and thoughtful and with a huge sense of fun which made her very popular with her friends. However, she also had a fiery temper – which was only equalled by Ferrars', and sometimes the very rafters shook with the fire and brimstone that was exchanged. Because I was brought up with Moo's bouts of utter exasperation over the latest act of absolute stupidity from Pa, I was inclined to take it all in my stride, probably feeling that most married couples probably behaved in this way when they were just *en famille*. Then, when I started actually weighing up the lives the Loftuses led, focusing on certain things for the first time – I noticed the strange position that 'Uncle John' Arbuthnot held in the household. Eventually Heather told me how Ferrars had invited John Arbuthnot to spend the weekend at Tingewick, Betty had taken a fancy to him – and he had never moved out![23] Ferrars, early on, decided that John Arbuthnot's presence at Tingewick could be used to his own advantage. Billie Fleck had been his very long-term mistress, a small elegant woman as totally different to plain but vivacious Betty as anyone on earth could be. It became the norm for Billie (and sometimes her quiet and very charming husband Bluey Fleck) to spend the weekend at Tingewick, along with another couple or two. Those weekend house parties were the essence of many of

---

[23] He actually stayed at Tingewick until Ferrars died in 1962 – and then removed himself forever, the day before his funeral, after making use of both Betty and Tingewick for over twenty years. He married a younger wealthy widow soon after that. You can imagine what both Geoff and Heather thought of him! [DV]

Britain's larger country house entertainments from the beginning of the 20th century, and the fact that Britain was very much at War when I was a guest there, seemed to have little impact on the gaiety of those occasions, let alone the ferocity of the thunderous rows that too much drinking invariable triggered. The parties became more frequent and outrageous when the USAAF arrived in England, bringing American music and supplies from a growing number of American bases around Buckingham.

Heather and I had taken to sharing her room so that we could chat through the night. As Heather and Geoff's rooms had a connecting door between them (they had started out as the day and night nurseries) the connecting door would frequently be left ajar and at first I would get very embarrassed by Geoff coming in and out to chat as we were going to bed. I took to getting undressed in the bathroom which solved my personal problem, which neither Heather nor Geoff seemed to have any idea about. Geoff was a very polite boy, but thoroughly enjoyed our night time gathering in Heather's room when everything was discussed, and it took me some time to come to realise how uncomfortable they found it to see their parents constantly at war with each other, sometimes in very public places. Nevertheless, it was hardly surprising that Tingewick was a rush of fresh air to a 14-year-old, offering unconditional acceptance to me, with a heady mix of music, forbidden alcohol and strange goings-on (abut which, aged 14, I hardly noticed or understood). But it also gives you some idea of the sort of life that both Geoffrey and Heather were raised into, explaining so very much about how they themselves matured. They both admitted to being ashamed of their parents' lifestyle and behaviour, while actually being fond of their father Ferrars, probably because Betty was always the one who misbehaved first.[24]

28 - Heather, who was distrusted "machines" and her father (Ferrars), who distrusted horses, expressing their fears in their own way.

Ferrars loved his machines, from had his own aeroplane (*The Bag*), to his Bentley cars. *The Bag* was a regular head-turner and naturally made many friends amongst the

---

[24] In her defence, Betty had been an only daughter with three brothers and two half-brothers. Her mother had died soon after she was born. She was very much indulged as a child, being brought up in the rarified atmosphere of great wealth by a father who started life as a successful Yorkshire mill owner, and went on to make several fortunes. He controlled much of Commercial Manchester in the first half of the 20th century and lived in a gracious and opulent stately home, Horton House, Horton, Northampton, filled with valuable treasures and cared for by a regiment of servants. Betty's only companion as she grew up was the head gardener's daughter Georgie Elliott, who then became her personal maid. Georgie went on to become the beloved 'Nanny'of both Geoff and especially Heather. [DV]

women pilots of the Air Transport Auxiliary. The ATA ferry pilot girls were an extremely courageous group of women who flew aircraft of all sizes throughout the 2nd World War, from the factories that created them to the airfields from which they would be operating. I will not go into the marvellous war record of these women here. You can read the ATA's history elsewhere, and a very illustrious history it is. But these women were all reasonably young, very experienced pilots and inclined to lead a hectic social life when they were not in the air. Their Headquarters was at White Waltham, near Maidenhead, and not far by air from where *The Bag* was kept at Kidlington. Ferrars had three regular 'partners'

29 - "The Bag", piloted by Enid Knight-Bruce

from this group, Enid Knight-Bruce, Vuvvie Watts (whose husband Charles was away on service duty in North Africa and then Italy), and Diana Barnato, daughter of his friend and fellow Bentley racing driver, the playboy Babe Barnato. I remember Babe quite well.

He was attractive in a beefy sort of way and a great party-goer. He spent many a weekend at Tingewick with, but mostly without, his American wife whose name escapes me. They divorced soon after the war and Babe then married the rather sweet Joan who had been his 'steady' extra wife for some time. Ferrars may well have had other, less regular companions but the ones I mention here are the only ones I can personally vouch for. Billie Fleck, whose real name was Doris, was his long-term steady until the day he died. Betty, who had to suffer the comments that were made about her relationship with John Arbuthnot, was always very pleasant to Billie during her visits, but behind her back Billie soon became known as 'The Wilting Whelk' (Betty's nickname for her) because she did tend to waft around in beautiful floaty clothes, looking ethereal and delicate, and needing lots of attention from the house staff. All the same, we three much preferred her to Betty's John – who had quite a light tenor voice with considerable affectation in the way he spoke. You could almost say that he was inclined to 'bleat'. He would also ill-treat Betty when he had had too much to drink and had thrown her out of his room on several occasions when she had 'gone to visit' him. As he was living free off the family and living extremely well too, we were generally disgusted with him, and also with Ferrars for allowing it to happen. Ferrars however, was not going to rock the boat because Betty could not object to Billie's visits while she herself had a live-in lover under their very roof. Little of this registered with me at the time but both Geoff and Heather bore the scars of those years of their upbringing, which ran deeply, affecting them both in quite different ways.

Neither had Betty and Ferrars' pretty *risqué* lifestyle gone unnoticed outside the family. In fact, many of the local 'Gentry' were inclined to ignore them as a consequence. Remembering the many photograph albums that Heather and I sometimes thumbed through to see how many 'famous' faces we could recognise, they illustrated the endless weekend house parties which was Tingewick's *chef d'oeuvre* between the two World Wars.

*

In the summer it was decided at school that they should produce an End of Year musical play. For some reason the three Music-teaching nuns got their heads together and chose an obscure operetta called 'Princess Ju-Ju'. In a way, it was a bit like a domestic version of Madam Butterfly without the need for such exotic stage furniture and backdrops. I had two parts to learn in this musical, in the chorus and in the lead role as Princess Ju-Ju. I did a lot of painting of stage scenery and absolutely loved that, but what really took up most of the time in the role as Princess Ju-Ju, and having to not only learn lines and do some acting, but I had three solos and the whole book to learn as part of the chorus. At first I was very worried and reluctant to agree to doing this part and Mother St Bernard was especially understanding, in view of my all-too-obvious fear of darkness and enclosed spaces. There were two occasions while I was on stage when I had to hide and I found it impossible to do that. I mastered the songs without trouble and my voice had actually improved and become a lot stronger as I grew older. But it was the acting side with a darkened stage on two occasions and then hiding under sacking painted to look like rocks. My body shook, I came out in a cold sweat, and on the first rehearsal I'm told that I momentarily passed out. Not being inclined to 'the vapours' by nature, I was ashamed of how my body was letting me down, but Heather showed her friendship most truly here. She had refused point blank to be anything at all in the play but, once she saw how the whole thing was not only affecting me but putting my whole role in jeopardy, she asked whether she could hide in the sacking 'rock' so that she could hold onto me when I had to be there. It worked beautifully and I was able to close my eyes and concentrate on the music, while feeling the reassurance of Heather's strong firm grip and her arm round my shoulder.

I suppose that I do not have as clear a memory of Princess Juju as I have of my first singing at the Convent at Hastings because I was still suffering quite badly from the after-effects of being buried so recently, but I do remember enough to know that the evening went well. Susie Cork took the part of my funny little attendant Lala. Princess Juju had several attendants but I only remember Susie who was in my class. She was small and very pretty with dark hair, flashing brown eyes and a wicked sense of humour. I think she made her part really amusing, more so than had been intended but it made the audience roar with laughter and enjoy the play all the more, which is what matters. Geoff was not in the audience, much to my relief, as it was becoming rather important for me to be at my best for him, and I was not sure whether this sort of part was quite my scene. Having written that, I realise with rather a shock that I have no memory at all of whether Pa and Moo were there or not – maybe their presence was no longer so important to me.

The evening was well supported and thoroughly enjoyed and because we were all dressed in lovely Japanese costumes made from every material under the sun, from curtains to paper, we had three memorable evenings when virtually the whole populace of the area turned out to support us. As the present cavernous school hall had not been built then, I guess that we could not accommodate more than about 150 people, so I can safely say that singing to 450 people was the largest audience I ever faced.

The first night was terrifying, the second less so – and by the third and last night we were all 'old hands' and marvellously comfortable in our parts. Susie brought the house down with her antics. I wonder if she ever became a comedienne? She should have, and being so small and delicious with that sort of humour would surely have appealed to the stoniest of audiences.

By Christmas of 1944 Moo's and my mental and physical damage must have been well on the road to recovery. Junie was still in a very fragile state, white as a sheet and almost unapproachable at times, but by the time I went back to school for the Spring Term in January 1945 she had been sent down to Portsmouth to have medical and remedial treatment which would gradually get her back to full duties. The WRNS quarters were in Southsea but eventually she was posted to worked the main Portsmouth dockyard, in Admiral Jack Tovey's office. Admiral Tovey was then Admiral of the Fleet, until he retired and moved to the Royal Household. I seem to recall that he had a distinct affection for Junie and always ensured that her duties were not too onerous while she was getting her health back. I wonder whether this might have been the moment when she began to drink, probably in order to keep up with her friends and work colleagues. I always hoped that it was not because of the attentions of Admiral Tovey! The fact that she was so outstandingly lovely to look at separated her slightly from her companions because she was always a target for male admiration; never able to creep away quietly. Popularity and being the centre of attention was almost forced on her so that gradually she became unable to do without it. She had not been that way as a child or even in her teens, because she had simply not been aware of the way she was beginning to flower then but, quite apart from her looks, she had such a fine brain with Pa's passion for detail and the exploration of any interesting subject. It was this fine-tuned mind of hers that suffered and starved because the men in her life were so bowled over by her looks and natural charm that they had no use for her mind. Time after time, the boyfriend of the moment tended to dismiss her opinions, her observations – so that she became frustrated not only with them but with her life. She reached for another glass….and then another glass to soften the edges of her dissatisfaction.

*

An extraordinary period of serenity welcomed the year 1945 for me. I suppose, looking back at the previous fourteen years, there had never really been much continuity or tranquillity. Life had been spent on the move, sometimes because of the war, sometimes because of our circumstances – and now and then because of me! The main ingredient for the change in me must have been Moo's and my Flying Bomb experience because, once I had recovered from the many effects it left, I became much more stable in myself, more thoughtful, less resentful. In short I began to grow up.

The Spring Term at Thornton college saw me at last becoming a weekly boarder at the school, having struggled through my first term by cycling to and fro each day. The Thornton Hall drive was, and still is, almost a quarter of a mile long and in those days it had a murderous surface of bumps and pot-holes which, if not negotiated with extreme care would have had me crashing to the ground. Added to that, my shoulders were still very weak and painful from their fractures and for some time I continued to arrive at school or back home in the evening in such pain that I was, now and then, not able to function for half an hour. Moo, with her own damaged body to concentrate on, did not seem to realise that this double cycle ride, though easier for me than walking both ways, was actually not doing my damaged shoulders any good. The nuns, especially Mother Annunciata, the saintly school nurse, and one of my favourite nuns there, were most concerned and I think they must have agreed to take me on as a weekly boarder for the same fees as a day-student. Whatever the politics there, I was so hugely relieved when Moo told me that I was to weekly-board from the first week in January that I crept away and had a little weep about the whole thing. To my great embarrassment, I welled up again the next day when I was called into Mother St. Dorothy's office and told with great kindness that I could return the bicycle to the school garage building because I would be staying at the school through the week and only returning home at weekends; and furthermore – and this is what did it - that the school car would drive me in both directions at weekends until my body was quite healed! I felt the tears prick in my eyes and spill down my face and I wanted so much to go and hug her in sheer gratitude, but of course you could not be so familiar with your Head Mistress, and so I just stuttered and gulped my thanks and the minute she let me go, rushed off to the school toilets in a cloud of happiness to mop my tears up.

From the time I went to Thornton and met Heather and Geoff, they became the centre of my life and from where I am now, it seems that I lost proper focus on Moo. This was quite selfish of me because, when you consider what had happened to Moo, I do not remember anyone paying any special attention to her or even considering the effects on her of the experience we had *both* suffered. I simply do not know what she did at Thornton Hall when I was at school or at Tingewick. The house was a longer walk from the road than she would ever have managed. She did not drive. I do not remember anything about buses. I wonder what she did all day? She was quite good friends with Nina Young, and very 'cordial' with Maudie Harris, but Pa was at Bletchley all day and Junie, once her breakdown began to lift, had been transferred to Portsmouth. How lonely my poor Moo must have been at Thornton.

I loved boarding at Thornton college. The school had fewer than one hundred pupils boarding at that time and so there were not floors of dormitories but an almost 'family' atmosphere. Since the house had been the Harris' home before the school had purchased it, I was given a cubicle in what must have been the Master bedroom, a huge room with about twelve beds in it, and with the most grotesque wallpaper on the walls. This room had obviously been lined with papers designed by William Morris and were probably so valuable that they were still on the walls in the 1940s. Imagine impossible climbing plants twisting and agonising up the walls, heavily shrouded in shades of greens and blues of every hue, with slimey-looking black tendrils everywhere, unexpectedly emphasised by sharp splashes of brilliant white; the agony of implied pain in every curled and tortured leaf and stamen. In an odd kind of way the design was so strong, so everlasting that maybe the gargantuan flowering creepers were an invisible encouragement to the young people who slept beneath them; children like me who had been bombed, starved, had their parents taken from them, and these extraordinary walls of tortured plant designs became our very strengths. Many of us had private mind games of climbing the thick stalks in search of that Utopia at the top of Jack's Beanstalk, and these nightly fantasies allowed us to sleep and block out the problems that so many of us carried around as a result of our experiences. I had a particularly lush bluey-white flower bud on the wall beside my bed in which Ian liked to curl up and wait for me to climb the spikey tendrils to join him. I therefore feel an element of affection for William Morris and his Arts and Crafts Group for helping to show me how to deal with my own problems.

I was given a corner bed, the first one you saw as you entered the room, which meant that I had Morris wallpaper on two sides, at the head of my bed and along the left side, so it was not long before I wrapped myself in the green protection of the trellis and snakelike leaves when I went to bed each night and would lie, safe in my exotic cocoon until sleep claimed me. I forget what our dormitory was called but the one at the other end of the corridor was called The Pink, and had the ten youngest children sleeping there. Their walls were covered in lovely soft pinkish buds and flowers creeping up the walls on a delicate trelliswork and were obviously intended for a little girl. All their beds had pink blankets (we had green ones) and the children all seemed marvellously happy there. Colour is an amazing tonic.

30 - Geoffrey Loftus 1945

It was during the spring term of 1945 that I actually felt the difference in myself. I did a lot more 'thinking' on my own, was able to give full voice to singing in the choir, which meant learning the joys of Plainsong or perhaps Gregorian Chants as those who know more about it than I do would call it. It is the way that monks and nuns sang in church from the earliest days of Christianity and I always absolutely loved the simplicity and pure beauty of the canticles. Out of this came various singing roles in school plays and it was Heather who told Geoff at this time that I was making a niche for myself in the choir. I remember him asking if I would like to sing something and he would play the melody. I was much too shy to do this at first, not only because I was shy of Geoff but because Tingewick was always full of people coming and going. One day, however, when I had gone over there with Heather for the weekend, Geoff was home and had been messing around on the piano in the drawing room, as he often did. Heather and I listened for a while, now and then asking him to play one tune after another. Heather suddenly suggested that he might play *Georgia on My Mind*, which Hoagie Carmichael had composed and recently recorded and which she and I particularly loved.

She gave me a nudge and said – "sing it!". I remember Geoff's grin of encouragement, felt my cheeks burning with the sheer embarrassment of singing to "a boy" – and then, as he picked up the melody so naturally and with such ease, the joy of the song came off the keys and in no time I relaxed and sang. *'Georgia on My Mind'* has always held a special magic for me from that day, even now.

I was fourteen years old – had had few dealings with boys in my life until then but here I was singing to Geoff – and it really *was* to him because I know that my eyes never left his until the song was finished, and I saw all kinds of expressions there; first of all surprise, then pleasure – then a sort of glow came into his face and I felt that my whole persona was absorbing the message in the music. We came to the end of the song and Heather clapped and banged the back of the Knowle sofa. "That was terrific – I told you she could sing." She said, but Geoff and I were grinning at each other like a couple of idiots.

'Other arms reach out to me - other eyes smile tenderly - still in peaceful dreams I see - The road leads back to you.'

That was the tune that wound itself around both the eighteen-year-old Geoff and the fourteen-year-old Dione and began to draw us towards each other from that time on.

At that time, there was a growing excitement with every news bulletin during that term and the children were encouraged to listen to the BBC broadcasts during our

31 - Dione Gordon-Finlay, 1945

211

free time. The Allies made steady, though bloody, progress through France, pushing back the German Front, which of course had been weakened by also having to sustain a Russian Front. Then on the 24th March Allied troops fought their way over the Rhine and into Germany itself – and the writing was on the wall. We were winning our War in Europe at long last.

On the 15th April the Western World was utterly horrified when British troops liberated the German concentration camp of Bergen Belsen and discovered the absolute outrage of what had been going on in that terrible death camp. I have in my head two pictures that were released to the newspapers (the rest were too horrific to be made public at that time) showing just a fraction of what the appalled and sickened British troops found behind the walls at Belsen. One was the image of a naked man sitting in a chair. He was absolutely skeletal but he had also been burned so that almost all that was left of him was skull and skeleton. The other picture was difficult to even look at; a huge pile of bodies in various stages of decomposition. Later reports told the tragic horror of the place where 10,000 corpses were counted. Another 60,000 emaciated humans, close to death, were treated by the British Army, the Red Cross, and Belgian Aid workers. Bulldozers had to be used to collect the typhus-infected bodies. The whole operation of clearing Belsen of its (just) living and its dead was one of the most appalling episodes of Germany's history, and was only the first of many more such nightmare discoveries such as Auschwitz, Buchenwald, and Dachau concentration camps. Some *seventy two* of these detestable death camps were discovered in all. Too many for discussion here but maybe it explains to you so many generations on from those days, the reason it

New Hope – VE Day

hardened the feeling of utter disgust for Germany from the rest of the Western World for many years afterwards. It also explains Germany's own sense of guilt and shame, which many do not understand today but which was very much justified amongst normal, God-fearing non-Nazi German people, of which there were many.

Suddenly, during the following summer term, everything began to happen all round us and few school lessons were either learned or even taught. On the 30th April Adolf Hitler, finally realising that his credit had run out, committed suicide in his bunker in Berlin shortly before the Allies arrived. On the 8th May, shortly after we had finished our evening soup with 'bread and scrape' we were hurried out of the refectory into the Common room where the wireless was already on and a group of nuns huddled close to it like a flock of blackbirds, listening intently. We sat on the floor and the volume was turned up so that we could all hear what was going on. There had been jubilant scenes in London earlier in the day when Germany had admitted defeat and now we heard the voice of Winston Churchill telling us that the second terrible war of the 20th century had been brought to a close in Europe by a triumphant Great Britain and her Allies, including the late but vital intervention of the United States.

In declaring Victory in Europe Day (we already knew it as VE day), Churchill told the cheering crowds "This is YOUR Victory!", delirious with relief and happiness below him, as he stood on the balcony of the Ministry of Health in Whitehall. He had been the most charismatic of Leaders of this small island in our darkest days, our emotional strength in the phraseology of his

213

stirring speeches, which were sometimes the only hope we had to cling onto, but it must have been very hard to lead a coalition government during those War years; a group of men and women with deeply opposing views. Churchill was already an old man. The very people he had led with such valiant determination would vote him out of office just two months after this wild and exhilarating day.

At Thornton college we were not concerned with politics. We were children; filled with the excitement of the moment and the joy of living, and the amazing truth that now we would have a chance to grow up normally, without fear – and with luck, without starvation. I went back to Tingewick with Heather that evening and the next morning we climbed up on the roof of the house with arms full of red, white and blue bunting and triangular flags and union jacks – and we decorated the chimneys and all the gutters – and that was the only time I remember getting (with Heather) furiously told-off by Ferrars.

He was quite right, of course. The roofs were high-pitched, the slate tiles old and inclined to crack and crumble – and slide away…. We had a very long way to fall had our feet slipped. Such, however, was our excitement at that time, adrenaline coursing in our veins, that this simply did not occur to either of us for a moment. It was our contribution to the celebrations.[25]

I'll never forget going upstairs with arms laden with bunting round our necks and bodies, and flags tucked

---

[25] I think the bunting came from years of the Annual Tingewick Garden Fete being held on the wide stretch of the upper and lower lawns in front of the house. [DV]

214

into our armpits. The way up was precarious; through the bedroom of Mabel the cook (without asking permission) into an attic in the eaves in the roof space, over which we had to pick our way from one joist to the next as there were no floorboards laid there, then out through a small door which allowed the gardner Jellyman to clear the gutters every year – and along a gully between two sloping roofs from east to west. We dumped most of our stuff there so that we could use both hands to balance ourselves going up the tiles. In order to reach the roof ridge we had to climb up the tiles to the front of the house so that we could decorate the three chimney stacks. It was a tricky bit of mountaineering, up the slippery old slates, where sometimes we could not avoid treading in the bird droppings so that our shoes shot sideways out of control. It did not help to, now and then, hear the slates cracking under our weight either. We edged our way along and up until we reached the comparative safety of the roof ridge, sat astride it and pulled ourselves along until we reached a chimney stack. Those chimneys were hugely high, Tudor-style chimneys and so Heather stood and held me and I, being lighter, balanced on the roof ridge and pushed and pulled until there was enough bunting, plus a flag, round the stack to show impressively from below. We did this on all the front stacks and then found we still had plenty of bunting left so we 'rode' our way along the roof ridge which jutted out three floors up over the front of the house and managed to hang out two Union Jacks and an American flag in honour of our AFN friends.

As there were still a couple of flags left and a bit of bunting, we threw them down to the gravel apron far below at the front of the house, planning to decorate the two pillars on either side of the front door. At this point the colourful bunting fluttering down past the study window attracted Ferrars, who was working at his desk. He shot out of the front door and, looking up, was horrified to see two happy girls straddling the distant roof ridge as though we were on bucking broncos.

He shook his fist at us. "Don't you dare to move one inch." He roared at us, face as purple as his nose. "Stay where you are. I'll get Jellyman to help you down. DON'T MOVE."

There was much banging of doors, furious cursing and shouting below, and Heather shrugged and began the careful business of moving backwards, away from the 'abyss' and back towards the comparative safety of the central gully between the two roofs. I had been in front of her, at the edge of the roof, but followed her backwards and we made it down to the gully floor in safety, the sun shining on us all the way. I had just got my feet back onto the lead of the gulley when the access door opened and Jellyman's head poked through. He looked at these two grimy girls with the stains and smells of generations of bird droppings, moss and other evil-smelling things all over us, beaming delightedly at him. "My word, you two are in for a blasting." Was all he'd say – and oh dear, we certainly were. It had not occurred to us that we could so easily have slipped and either broken some part of ourselves, or even worse. Fourteen and sixteen then were not the mature ages that they seem to be today. We were still children, in so many ways, even if more adult emotions were just beginning to stir in us.

Ferrars was, under his weather-beaten skin, quite white-faced and shaken by the time we returned to ground level. His moustache almost bristled with anger, the drained colour of his cheeks emphasised by the perennial beacon of his extremely red nose. For one terrible moment I had to button my mouth or I would have burst out laughing. A recent Christmas song had filtered across from America called *Rudolf the Red-nosed Reindeer* and the similarity suddenly hit me as we were being read the Riot Act so that I had to lower my eyes and study my scuffed, guano-smelling shoes. I did indeed understand how scary it must have looked to Ferrars, but I was still too young to have my budding self-confidence reduced by his righteous anger. Heather apologised for us both, I muttered my own regret and we both did our best to look hang-dog, but the adrenaline was still flowing - we were at the beginning of our lives, the War was over and we could not imagine that anything we did might have put an end to us before we'd had a chance to enjoy the years ahead.

Predictably, Betty was greatly amused when she heard what we had done – and viewed our handiwork with approval. "If I'd been there, I'd have helped you." She said, smiling at us both between furious puffs at her cigarette. She always smoked fast when something stimulated her. As she was very often stimulated, one way or another, she did a great deal of smoking. The house looked pretty good though, all decked out in red white and blue. Jellyman was instructed to help us to finish the job with crossed-flags on the pillars either side of the front door, and we were then shooed away to clean ourselves up because there was to be a special service of thanks-giving at the church next door that evening and WE WOULD BE ATTENDING IT.

217

We had, of course, been at school when Peace was announced a couple of days before, and all the church bells in the land pealed out a message of joy and thankfulness. The nuns had been happy for the little Thornton church to give its own celebratory peon to Victory, and how marvellous it must have been for the people of these Islands to hear these ancient bells filling the air as they rang out from one end of the British Isles to the other on that day, the first time the bells had rung since war had been declared over five and a half years earlier.

32 – "Authorised" VE-Day celebrations, nursery window, Tingewick Hall April 8th, 1945

AFTERWORD

War had shattered our lives but had also brought us together; peace scattered our lives. Heather was sent to finishing school, I studied for my music exams and scraped through them without distinction, Junie left the WRNS to attend Art School and Geoff was sent to Germany to do his military service. As my body and mind healed from its battering in 1944, I became aware of the calming effect the whole experience had had on me. Moo and I had fewer battles, Pa suddenly began to look like an elderly man with the fizz and sparkle draining out of him, though not yet sixty. All the same, at that particular moment we began to recognise the tell-tale signs that he had the beginnings of something new and exciting brewing in his head. He was clearly finding it difficult to work at Bletchley Park by then, and indeed they must have realised this as he was 'retired' and in a flash he was off to Switzerland like a rocket, to open up the house, and to get stuck into whatever was beginning to eat away at him. We all knew those signs – and Moo was only too happy for him to go ahead of us. I was torn between longing to see our home again and aching to pass my exams to get on with the start of my adult life. With Pa leaving Bletchley Park it meant that we were no longer eligible for the Thornton flat. The lease came to an end in mid-August. Pa went back to Switzerland in July and because it was taking time for the Passport Office in Petit-France, London, to process our passports (Junie and I had been on Moo's passport but now we had to have our own), we would have to stay in a London hotel until all the paperwork had been cleared.

The day came, a couple of weeks before Christmas of 1945, when Moo at last had all the appropriate paperwork. I have been trying to remember which ferry took us across the channel because many of the French ports were still too war-damaged to operate. I think we went via Newhaven to Dieppe and I see that this line had indeed *just* begun to operate again that Autumn. I know we disembarked after a terrible choppy winter crossing which meant that my childhood's unreliable stomach had not improved one bit and, having emptied the contents of my entire self throughout the crossing, I was hardly able to stagger after Moo and Junie as they joined the queue to pass through Customs. I do not even remember getting on the train to Paris – or how we got from the Gare du Norde to the Gare de Lyon. There are cameo snatches of that long tortuous journey on the Simplon line that are still here with me though; the clammy cold of the unheated carrriages, the lumpy, stale-smelling, uncomfortable seats, the odour all round us of sickly, unwashed bodies – and the coffee available on the train, which was apparently made from acorns. Whatever it was, it was terribly bitter – but it was hot and wet.

My rolling stomach must have come to its senses over the next sixteen hours because flashes of those hours roll into my head, of the over-crowding, the pinched white French faces round me with their hollow eyes, made huge by the dark smudges of their exhaustion. We thought that we in Britain had had a bad time in the war, but the French had been invaded, its people and lands desecrated *twice* in thirty years and they were, as a Nation, in a state of mental and physical exhaustion. Time passed so slowly because the train crept and rattled over worn points, and kept stopping where the rail track was under repair. We must have stopped for this reason at least fifteen to twenty times, and as the train also stopped to pick up and put down passengers in both Amiens and Lyons (where we seemed to linger forever) we felt we must be traveling the whole length of this tortured and disseminated Country. Gradually our squashed limbs became stiff with no use, sitting pressed against the next person, who might well have been carrying their entire possessions on their laps, or nursing an unhappy, hungry baby. Junie had a window seat and sat glued to whatever was passing us outside, but Moo and I had places between two other people and so could not even say much to each other. When we did, the fact that we were speaking English usually drew darkly suspicious glares from our companions so that, eventually we hardly said a word. I sank into a long dream about Geoff, trying to push away the fact that I was bursting to go to the loo but, having discovered the state of the only toilet in our carriage, would rather have burst my bladder than risk even opening its door!

By the time we finally screeched to a juddering, squealing halt and were told that this was as far as the line could take us, we were deep into another black night. We had become disoriented by the jerky, snail's pace of our shambling progress and the monotonous rolling rattle of our train over damaged and badly-repaired tracks, through empty, violated villages, untilled fields whose crops had been destroyed, forests pulverised by explosions and fire, mountains rearing up starkly against a dull sunset, edged in an early dusting of snow, gauntly sentinel against so much destruction. It was a relief when the day died and night with a new sprinkling of fine light snow closed in on us. As we all sat forward a little, wondering why we had stopped once again, a train guard and two officials pushed their way along the length of the train corridors, through those who had to stand, calling into each compartment that we had reached our destination and that the rail came to an end at this point, and to leave the train by our outer compartment doors. I still feel that by-now familiar sense of loss when we were ordered out of the train, the odourous few inches surrounding us which had become the only reality in the hours of our slow and tortuous journey. There was general sluggish movement as everyone stood up, stretching and groaning from the stiffness of limbs, the uncertainty of what was still ahead. We gathered ourselves and our belongings and, dull and obedient as sheep, lowered ourselves from the carriage doorway, down into the darkness, onto the verge beside the rails. We finally saw why it had been important not to overload ourselves and were thankful that our main luggage had been sent by freight which, in those days in France meant enormous carts drawn by huge shire horses since a national shortage of petrol meant that France's desperate situation at that time was a lot worse than ours.

We clamboured down from the train, dropping the last foot or so onto a sloping embankment and poor Moo, legs weak from sitting without exercise for too long, lost her balance in the darkness and fell, rolling out of sight into the night.

"Hold this." Junie thrust her case into my hands. "And DON'T MOVE," and she scrambled down the bank in the direction Moo had disappeared. People pushed past me, tripped over Junie's case, muttered darkly, a few choice curses were aimed at me – and then, night vision gradually giving me clearer sight, I saw the two of them, dishevelled as ruffians, pulling themselves back up the embankment onto the railway line, where I stood guard over our cases. Moo's hat had disappeared and her hair, so neat and tidy always, looked as though she had had a night out with a gorilla – but she was still holding her blue dress case and, apart from a scratch down one cheek, she seemed to have survived her fall without damage. I went to hug her; my poor little Moo who never did things like falling down railway embankments, but she gave me a quick rueful smile and, obviously unhurt, shushed me on ahead of her. We joined the rest of the crowd trailing along the embankment and began to pick our way beside the rails until they disappeared and then there was just the embankment path and black night all round us.

I cannot seem to comprehend the actual time that this all took in the dark chill of night but eventually the narrow track widened to a small 'halt' where farmers loaded their milk churns into the rear guards vans of passing trains in better days. An official with a torch came down the straggling procession of humanity, with a word here and there and a great many gestures. It seemed that we would have to walk along the empty track for about two kilometres, which is about a mile and a half. The Germans had intentionally removed the rails for this distance to the Franco-Swiss border in a deliberate attempt to stop food and medical supplies being brought in from Switzerland.

I don't know how long it took us to make that walk. We realised why we had been told in London to wear good strong walking shoes and thick winter coats. Junie and I had a scarf each to cover our heads but Moo had insisted on wearing a hat – and this had gone when she fell out of the train. I had put around my neck a warm woolly scarf that I had been forced to knit at school, and which I had finally finished and become quite fond of. It was striped yellow and green and was so narrow that it was more like a six foot long woolly cravat. I removed my treasured handiwork from round my neck and put it round Moo's head to keep the almost invisible snow-flakes from making her hair even wetter. She wound it round and round her head and then round her neck and tucked it into the top of her coat. "Well, I always realised your knitting took on a lot of odd shapes," She said as we followed the shadowy crowd around us, "but I never thought I'd bless your design sense until now, Darling." She gave a little giggle, looking like an Indian football supporter in her green and yellow knitted turban. We three grinned at each other and somehow felt a lot better because her special sense of humour, not often in evidence recently, could still ease the tension.

It seemed a very long cold night before there was a stir of excitement some distance ahead, from those moving forward around us; the pace picked up with shapes at last appearing out of the damp gusty night and we all moved towards a distant light, fuzzy and indistinct from the fine snow that billowed round us. Eventually we came to a halt where a whole necklace of lights fanned out far ahead, from left to right for as far as we could see. The Border at Vallorbe.......... Someone near me hushed a small child who had been sobbing for some time and gradually we inched forward; stopped – and then inched forward a few more steps, our bodies trembling with the deepening cold by this time. Our noses felt like blocks of ice stuck to our rigid faces; the snowflakes swirled and danced over us, around us, cloaking our heads and shoulders with melting white frosting. Shivering, we stamped our feet and I gave Moo and then Junie a "Hot Potato" which I had learned to do at Thornton. You press your mouth to the person's back and breathe out deeply so that the hot breath from your lungs seeps through coats, jumpers, vests and anything else before the skin of the back finally glows with the delicious, short-lived, warmth of it. "Mmmm", Moo said, leaning in rapture against me. "I'm glad the nuns succeeded in teaching you *something* useful at Thornton"

We shuffled, an almost invisible chain-gang towards the lights, step by step in the thinning darkness and it seemed an age had passed before at last we realised that the French/Swiss frontier building at Vallorbe was right ahead of us. Behind it, invisible at that moment, the railway tunnel burrowed its way under the mountains and emerged in Lausanne on its dividing way south, through to Geneva and north to the Capital Berne. I had already travelled this route several times in my life as we had always spent our summers in England, re-bonding with Moo's and Pa's families, but it had now been nearly seven years since we had last been this way.

The relief as we filed slowly into the Frontier building and felt the warmth of clean central heating enfolding us, to see glowing yellow lights ahead, clean smart uniforms on the Swiss officials and smiling, well-fed faces all round us was too much for Moo. She wept quietly to herself as we had our passports stamped and the official said to her – "Welcome back to Switzerland Madame Finlay." He was an elderly man, and had seen from our passports how often she had been coming and going over the years. Maybe he had even recognised Moo and her daughters from before 1939, but the welcome was a real sign of our arrival for Moo, and she beamed radiantly at him with the tears falling, and thanked him, her face alive with happiness, her French as fractured as it always was.

We were processed within half an hour and would not have minded if it had taken the rest of the night because we were once more warm and the air was clean and sweet-smelling and there was plenty of room to sit. Most important of all, the toilets were fresh and plentiful and a team of cleaners ensured that, despite the desperate state of most of us, those toilets remained sweet-smelling and shining with cleanliness throughout the desperate dash that several hundred exhausted travellers made to relieve themselves. There was a long queue but also plenty of comfortable seats and as time passed and we waited our turn, we simply absorbed the utter relief, the exhausted happiness we felt and could see in the faces of all those around us. And then our names were called. We stood up and followed Moo, clutching our cases and as we came through the barrier to the main entrance hall, there was Pa, cadaverous face grinning from ear to ear, his blue eyes dancing with excitement, waving both arms. It was such a supreme relief to see someone so entirely familiar there. It brought the whole journey into focus, giving its grinding endless distance a purpose, now at last complete. We were home and all of us were together. The details of the grinding journey lost focus, became a blur. They no longer mattered.

After an emotional greeting which our exhaustion made curiously quiet, Pa guided us to the cafeteria where, because the time must now have been in the region of 4 or 5 in the morning, we would have breakfast before boarding the Lausanne-Bernese Oberland train. The three of us were worn out, especially Moo, whose internal injuries from the previous year made it difficult for her to hold her suitcase, so that Junie and I had taken it in turn to carry it for her. Our departure from Victoria station in London already felt as though we had left another life behind a long time ago. We had shifted from hotel to train to ship, to train, across Paris to another station and then more train. The long, rattlingly slow journey over France's decimated rail system, followed by that almost sightless trudge through mud and billowing snow with our suitcases, over terrain that we could not even see, apart from the people immediately in front of us: all this was made the more worrying at the time because we'd had absolutely no idea of what to expect of the next step in our journey, but had to rely on the French railway officials who were few and far between. Those we did question had seemed as exhausted as we were, and the acorn coffee must have made them short of temper because they were, to a man, snappy and exasperated whenever they were questioned. The young Dione only saw their irritability and felt that they did not like us because we were British but, looking back, it must have been a terrible job, having to explain why the train moved so slowly, where the dangers lay and why the tracks were unreliable. Most of all, they must have felt how lucky we, *Les Anglaise*, were to be getting to Switzerland at all when they'd endured a much worse war in France than we had had in The United Kingdom.

I will never forget that breakfast. How could any of us, after years of bread and scape, suddenly having the sumptuous splendour and delicate fragrance of fresh hot croissants, brioche which melted in the mouth, a dish piled with neat squares of glorious pure Swiss butter, a bowl of unforgettable Swiss Black Cherry Jam – and the almost overpowering glory of the aroma that came from a large pot of freshly ground coffee................. The whole room became hushed, apart from small sounds of pure contentment. Pa let us wallow in that breakfast, watching us, no doubt remembering when he had done the same wondrous thing, having flown into Geneva a few months before. I cannot remember how long we managed to string out that amazing breakfast experience. I know we all ate more than our shrunken stomachs could deal with and I finished my umpteenth croissant with a distinctly queasy feeling which, without doubt, was well worth the discomfort. The Lausanne train was announced and we gathered our possessions and left that warm and glowing shrine as dawn lightened the Swiss skies. We sat in comfortable, well-upholstered seats in a clean and freshly–painted train compartment and, as we moved into the Simplon tunnel and the carriage lights dipped, relaxed back into the blissful embrace of our seats – and missed the whole trip through to Geneva because sleep claimed us immediately, as though a light had been switched off in every one of us.

New Hope – VE Day

It was an unbelievable joy to be home. Even now, it is difficult to find the words to express the relief of being in our very own property, rather than someone else's, and to know that it had not been damaged by bombs or allowed to fall into disrepair because of the lack of materials, or that we could no longer afford to live in it. Everything about Switzerland seemed to radiate well-being, to glow with 'care' – we were surrounded by a country that had, during the War, continued to trade in every direction because it was not part of this dreadful destructive and often bestial conflict. It had seen fit to do business with both sides of the struggle and had benefitted supremely throughout the six years when countryside and human beings were being annihilated on every one of its frontiers.

Our cook/housekeeper Edda had disappeared and we never discovered what had happened to her. Maybe she had become one of those who had died when visiting relations in Germany or France, or even Italy. Pa had talked to the family who still ran the boulangerie in Claie aux Moines and they produced Rosa, who had spent weeks cleaning and refreshing our poor abandoned house, so that by the time we arrived back at L'Avendue it was waiting for us with the same familiar sandalwood polish scent in the air, and even the feeling of welcome and permanence that had always been my greatest rock. My old bedroom still had the doll's house, toys and books that a very much younger Dookie had made her own, and I stood in the middle of that room, taking everything in, knowing that I had long outgrown all these child's treasures and maybe realising just how deep the absence of continuity had affected those growing-up years which were now behind me.

L'Avendue and then Tingewick were the only stable homes that I had ever experienced, apart from the London flat which we only used occasionally – and that had gone now. The War years had seen us tossed like leaves on a stormy sea, into move after move, and drama after drama. Enough, surely, to affect the minds of everyone, and it must indeed have scarred us all, though I did not see that at the time. The odd thing was that all the moving around, all the fear and the 'near-misses' (I think of our cancelled places to Canada in the *City of Benares* here) and those nightmare hours under the rubble of the Beckenham house seemed to have actually stabilised me, because I had stopped being a constant nuisance, had learned to control the rebellious streak and no longer felt the need to be a law unto myself.

33 - Geoff came to see Dione at L'Avendue, 1946

We had a blissful Christmas that year and to my great delight, Geoff came out to stay with us when he had some leave. He was with us for ten days and during that time the beauty of our surroundings and the calm happiness of us all at L'Avendue cast its spell over the two of us. Moo did her best to bring in other young people from nearby families that we had known before the war, but it was all too clear that we British and Swiss youngsters had done our growing up in two sectors that had little to do with each other – that of living through a war of death and destruction, food shortage and the grief of loss – and that of watching what was going on all round you without any of the actual privations. They had always been terrified that Germany would simply march in and take Switzerland over one day, but the little country had proved to be more useful, as were Spain and Portugal, by keeping out of the conflict and allowing the through passage of the enemies, acting as a kind of "No Man's Land". I can understand how insecure this must have felt to the Swiss, but they were all healthier and fatter than we were and the difference showed all too clearly.

*

Moo tried to get me interested in being "finished-off" in Geneva but I was set on returning to England and going to The Central School of Speech and Drama, located at The Albert Hall at that time. For once, Pa seemed to agree that this would be worth trying, and before more could be said, arranged for me to stay with those patient and kindly cousins at Kensington Square. Eventually a vacancy came up for me in the flat that Junie and her friends had taken in St. George's Square, Pimlico and that is where I settled. I lost no time in returning to Tingewick to catch up with Heather who had now completed her year at finishing school and felt no more polished by it than she had been when she left Thornton college. We had endless laughs comparing finishing experiences, and triumphantly assured each other that, if anything, we were probably even less 'refined' than we had been before. I was drawn ever closer to Tingewick, where Heather had taught me to ride and now Ferrars was teaching me to fly.[26] When Geoff returned from Germany, we became inseparable and in 1947, were secretly engaged. The war years had been formative for me but what followed were years of joy and crisis, growth and death that were the equal to those war years and just as life affirming.

---

[26] I registered over 400 pilot hours in my logbook, mostly in *The Bag*, but also flying a neighbour's Auster. [DV]

INDEX

K

L

M

N

O

P